LIFELONG LEARNING ON THE INFO

SERIES EDITOR: JUDITH M. ROBE

Compressed Video Learning

Creating Active Learners

JUDITH M.
Roberts

Chenelière/McGraw-Hill
MONTRÉAL • TORONTO

Compressed Video Learning
Creating Active Learners

Judith M. Roberts

Project coordinator: Gertrude D'Urso
Copy editor: Jane Pavanel
Proofreader: Geraldine Kikuta
Typesetting: Julie Leclerc
Cover: Opus House and Norman Lavoie
Illustrations: Norman Lavoie

Canadian Cataloguing in Publication Data

Roberts, Judy

Compressed video learning: creating active learners

(Lifelong learning on the information highway)

Includes bibliographical references.

ISBN 2-89461-196-X

1. Teleconferencing in education. 2. Video tapes in education. 3. Videoconferencing. I. Title. II. Series.

LB1044.75.R62 1998   371.33'58   C97-941498-9

Chenelière McGraw-Hill

Chenelière/McGraw-Hill
7001 Saint-Laurent Blvd.
Montréal (Québec)
Canada H2S 3E3
Telephone: (514) 273-1066
Fax: (514) 276-0324
chene@dlcmcgrawhill.ca

ISBN 2-89461-196-X

Legal deposit: 1st quarter 1998
Bibliothèque nationale du Québec
National Library of Canada

Printed in Canada by AGMV Marquis Imprimeur inc.
1 2 3 4 5 02 01 00 99 98

TABLE OF CONTENTS

Acknowledgments

This book benefits from the generous support of a number of people. Instructors shared their stories; manuscript reviewers contributed their time and expertise; and colleagues always responded when asked for assistance. Jamie Rossiter, Scott Duncan and Liz Radojkovic know why they merit special thanks.

A number of organizations gave critical support. Laurentian University transferred copyright of a book prepared for its faculty; Part 3 is based heavily on material Thérèse Lamy and the author originally wrote for the University's Centre for Continuing Education. Vendors provided access to visual materials and clients. Trifolium Books Inc. transferred ownership of an earlier version of the manuscript.

Any errors or omissions that remain are entirely the responsibility of the author.

Judy Roberts

PREFACE

This book, entitled *Compressed Video Learning: Creating Active Learners,* is an integral part of the *Lifelong Learning on the Information Highway*™ Series.

GOALS

This Series is designed for professionals who want to use learning technologies in ways that facilitate the interdependent functions of learning and communication. More specifically, the Series will enable you to:

- know why learning professionals are using these technologies
- master the basic details you need to know to use the equipment appropriately
- learn from the successes of a range of public and private sector organizations throughout the world
- design, deliver and evaluate presentations that use the technologies effectively

You should feel comfortable with the idea of facilitating learning and communication by the time you have finished reading each book in the Series. They have been designed as a starting point, however, and not as a final destination. To that end, each book contains Further Readings for you to pursue if you are interested.

APPROACH

The Series reflects practitioners' experiences and relies heavily on original, unpublished material that reflects current practice in the public and private sectors. Many personal communications from practitioners and researchers have been gathered and appear in quotation marks throughout the book but have not been referenced by date. An informal style is used to describe these practitioners, so that the reader knows their full name, title and organizational affiliation. Where the authors know the practitioners personally, first names are often used after the first use of their full names.

Published quotes are cited by date in the text and are fully referenced in the References section at the end of each chapter. Contact information is provided for all practitioners whose stories are included in the book so that you may get in touch with them by mail, telephone, fax or e-mail to learn more about their work.

The Series shows how each technology can be used separately; it also integrates the technologies and prepares you, as the classroom instructor, for their convergence although they are now often considered distinct. Particularly pertinent points are prominently displayed in the margin.

CONTENT

The Series addresses the issue of how to facilitate learning in a classroom equipped with one or more of compressed video, computer and/or audio or audiographic learning technologies. It consists of four titles.

- *Classrooms with a Difference: Facilitating Learning on the Information Highway* (2nd Edition) integrates three key aspects of the new classroom: learners, models of course or workshop design and their application to interactive, distributed technologies. It emphasizes the first two elements and provides an introduction to each of the three technologies that are the subject of separate books in the Series.
- *Audio and Audiographic Learning: The Cornerstone of the Information Highway* reminds us of the potential offered by audio and audiographic technologies, both in their own right and as basic skills for other approaches.
- *Networked Learning: The Pedagogy of the Internet* introduces the basic tools and strategies you need to create learning opportunities through computer networks.
- *Compressed Video Learning: Creating Active Learners* describes instructional techniques that produce interactive learners in classrooms or at desktops.

FORMAT

The Series integrates multi-mode materials chosen to suit the needs of each book.

Modularized print is the foundation of the Series, since we believe it is still the most widely available learning technology. This book is divided into three parts, each of which contains chapters designed to answer common questions about the book's topic. Each part and each chapter is as self-contained as possible so that you can read them in whatever order responds to your needs and learning style. For example, your first priority may be to find out who is active in the field, or you may want to know how to use Compressed Video Learning. We encourage you to proceed through the book in an order that makes sense to you; don't feel constrained by our structure.

The Series also contains an appropriate blend of resources other than print and uses technology to teach technology: for example, a videotape illustrates the manual on Audio and Audiographic Learning and a computer disk supplements the guide on Networked Learning.

THE READER

This Series was developed as an introductory tool for instructors in the public and private sectors who have practical experience in teaching but who are novice users of technology. Designed primarily for a broad audience of instructors beyond the traditional distance learning community, each book covers practice, theories and research that administrators, learning designers and evaluation specialists will find helpful.

Readers from both the public and private sectors are addressed in this Series because many applications involve partnerships between schools, colleges, universities, government and business—partnerships that often transcend national boundaries. We hope to enhance such collaborations within and across the public and private education and training sectors by providing a common platform for understanding the learning and training potential of the Information Highway. Additional specialized resources are referenced so that readers in each sector can pursue its unique interests in more detail.

TERMINOLOGY

We believe that the term *Information Highway* refers to all information and communications technologies, not just the Internet. We therefore include several types of technologies in this Series and refer often to other learning technologies not dealt with to date as separate titles in the Series.

Jargon-free language is used in a conversational writing style throughout all the books in the Series. Inclusive language is used wherever possible. The term *instructor,* for example, is employed since we find that it is less directly associated with a given sector than *teacher* or *professor.* We use instructor to mean a person who facilitates active learning in a variety of ways, not someone who is a conveyer of content through lectures. The terms *learner* and *participant* are used for a similar reason. Exceptions occur when quoting specific examples where the word *professor* or *student* is appropriate to the case study being described. Sometimes, the instructor's role is so clearly that of a moderator or facilitator that those terms may be employed.

Where technical terms are unavoidable, they are used and included in a Glossary at the end of the book.

WORKSHOPS

The *Lifelong Learning on the Information Highway*™ team is available to assist you in designing workshops and other types of learning activities based on the Series. The team will customize workshops to meet your specific needs or act as resource people in sessions that you design. In addition to the books and multi-mode learning materials described in this Preface, a set of "workbooks for workshops" is available based on the Series.

LEARNER'S GUIDE

A Learner's Guide is also available as part of the Series. It contains a chapter on each of Networked, Audio, Audiographic and Compressed Video Learning. Nineteen learners were interviewed as the Guide was written; their stories and advice to other learners are the Guide's key resource.

INTRODUCTION

Videoconferencing, a technique that uses conventional television broadcast technology interactively, dates to approximately the 1950s, notes Robert Lochte (1993), a professor at Murray State University in Kentucky. Compression of the video signal through digital technology has become a practical possibility only in the 1990s, as Barbara Hakes and her co-authors (1993, 1995) have stated in their two books on compressed video published by The Association for Educational Communications and Technology. Nevertheless, there is a growing group of public and private sector professionals throughout the world who use compressed video conferencing equipment successfully for education and performance support. Their experience is the basis for this book.

Compressed Video Learning (called Video Learning throughout this book) refers to the learning that occurs when instructors and learners use microphones, cameras and other digital videoconferencing equipment to exchange verbal and moving color images to engage in discussion, share messages and talk to experts as part of a formal or informal learning process. All such activities occur in real-time; the instructors and learners are present at different sites at the same time and must coordinate their schedules. Compressed videoconferencing equipment reduces the "space" (and thus the cost) normally required to transmit a television signal (picture plus sound). Since the capital and operational costs of compressed videoconferencing are lower than those of conventional broadcast technology, institutions can afford to purchase and operate the equipment, and enrich the learning process by enabling participants to see and hear one another in real-time.

Together with the companion videotape, this book is designed to help you begin the process of becoming a skilled facilitator of effective Video Learning. Part 1 highlights the opportunities offered by Video Learning, reviews the fundamentals of how the equipment works and describes the resources you will need to access it, with a particular focus on technical, physical and financial considerations. The videotape expands the book's print description with moving color pictures of different types of videoconferencing equipment. Part 2 presents 15 examples of Video Learning drawn from schools, colleges, universities and workplaces in Canada and abroad. People from some of these success stories describe other aspects of their work on the videotape. Part 3 enables you to consider planning, delivery and evaluation issues and helps you decide how to apply them in your own environment.

We took a team-based approach when preparing this book. We talked to a broad range of people such as managers, learning designers, vendors, technical staff and evaluation specialists because we believe that instructors need to understand how their colleagues can enrich the Video Learning process. In the same spirit, we included public and private sector experience drawn from North America, Europe and Australia. As cross-sectoral and international partnerships become increasingly common, they will prosper better, we feel, if they share a common platform of understanding.

Now that you have a sense of how this book and videotape are organized, we invite you to start with whatever topic interests you the most, or whatever format is most appropriate to your learning style.

References

Hakes, B. T., Sachs, S. G., Box, J., & Couchenour, J. (1993). *Compressed video: Operations and applications*. Washington, DC: The Association for Educational Communications and Technology.

Hakes, B., Couchenour, J., Rezabek, L., & Sachs, S. (1995). *Compressed video for instruction: Operations and applications*. Revised and enlarged. Washington, DC: The Association for Educational Communications and Technology.

Lochte, R. H. (1993). *Interactive television and instruction*. Englewood Cliffs, NJ: Educational Technology Publications.

PART 1

WHAT IS COMPRESSED VIDEO LEARNING?

Part 1 lays the foundation for the balance of the book. Chapter 1 is designed to enable you to decide when and why you should use Compressed Video Learning, alone or in combination with other approaches. It also offers you a review of common misconceptions about Video Learning and how to overcome resistance if you have been asked to advocate its use in your organization. Chapter 2 provides a jargon-free overview of the technology and is supplemented by material on the videotape. Chapter 3 describes communication, space, human and financial issues that have to be considered in developing a business plan for Video Learning. As a group, these chapters set the context for the learning issues that are the focus in Parts 2 and 3.

Chapter 1

When and Why Should I Use Video Learning?

It's exciting to be a pioneer, seizing the opportunities which new tools such as videoconferencing offer to us: i.e., the chance to look at new possibilities and new ways of doing things. Too often we look backwards and want to do things the same old way.

DIANA HENSHAW,
CONTINUING STUDIES, EAST CAROLINA UNIVERSITY,
GREENVILLE, NORTH CAROLINA

INTRODUCTION

When you have finished reading this chapter, you will know when to choose Video Learning in addition to, or instead of, other learning strategies. You will also know how Video Learning relates to other learning and training approaches such as Audio and Audiographic Learning and Networked Learning. You will understand the particular strengths and weaknesses of Video Learning, common misperceptions, reasons why people resist it and strategies to overcome that resistance.

WHAT IS COMPRESSED VIDEO LEARNING?

Compressed Video Learning occurs when instructors and learners use microphones, cameras and other digital videoconferencing equipment to exchange verbal and moving color images to engage in a variety of formal or informal learning activities. Other terms sometimes used to describe this activity include interactive television or interactive videoconferencing. For convenience, we will use the term *Video Learning* throughout the balance of the book. Sometimes, terms such as videoconferencing are used to describe equipment configurations that are different from those treated here. For example, researchers Paul Biner, Kimberly Welsh, Natalie Barone, Marcia Summers and Raymond Dean (1997) at Ball State University examined one-way television with two-way audio and labeled the technology "interactive telecourses" and televised instruction. Other times, such as in Thomas Westbrook's article (1997), it is difficult, if not impossible, to know what type of interactive television is being used.

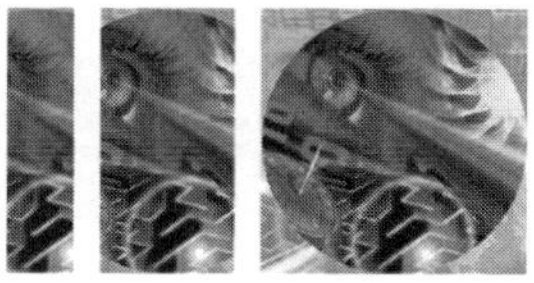

BECAUSE OF THESE VARIATIONS IN TERMINOLOGY AND EQUIPMENT, IT IS IMPORTANT TO LEARN ENOUGH ABOUT THE TECHNOLOGY TO ENSURE THAT WHAT YOU ARE READING IS PERTINENT TO YOUR TECHNICAL ENVIRONMENT. CHAPTER 2 GIVES YOU THE TECHNICAL KNOWLEDGE YOU NEED TO MAKE SUCH A JUDGMENT.

WHEN SHOULD I USE VIDEO LEARNING?

Instructors typically decide to use Video Learning for one or more reasons. The following list, adapted from a guide prepared by Transport Canada's Training Directorate in 1993, illustrates typical objectives:

1. to build a sense of direct involvement and "physical presence" among geographically dispersed learners

2. to permit participants to learn as well as, or better than, they do when using other learning methods and technologies
3. to offer participants at distant sites access to live, interactive learning opportunities
4. to deliver global expertise to learners in central or remote sites
5. to eliminate or reduce travel time and time away from jobs and family for instructors and learners
6. to generate revenue by including new audiences in a learning event
7. to create efficiencies, cost savings and value for money in delivering learning
8. to develop partnerships among public and private sector stakeholders from around the world

Video Learning has both strengths and limitations as a learning support tool. Video Learning permits:

1. the development of a sense of presence and cohesion among participants
2. the sharing of a wide variety of visual resource materials
3. the application of learning formats such as role playing, demonstrations and simulations

Unless the more expensive types of technology are used, Video Learning does not generally:

1. transmit clear pictures of rapid movements
2. permit visual materials with very fine print or detail to be read easily
3. strengthen the learning of factual material unless the content requires a visual demonstration

Moreover, compressed videoconferencing technology demands from users a bit of practice to adapt to the brief delay in voice transmission.

There are ways to compensate for these restrictions, however. For example, factual material can be presented by Video Learning as long as the lecture mode is not overused. Evaluation results from the University of Calgary's graduate course in engineering indicate that both instructors and students need to be aware of, and use, features such as interactivity. Ms. Urmil Chugh (1993), the course evaluator, noted in her report that instructors need in-service (training) that discusses the capacity of the technology, its interactivity and the need to modify traditional classroom teaching styles. She noted that the students who changed their learning strategies to adapt to the interactivity of videoconferencing felt more motivated and more in control of their learning needs than those who did not.

Skills can be acquired and assessed if Video Learning sessions are supplemented by off-line time slots designed for activities in which learners can practice while being observed by qualified mentors and evaluators. A number of other strategies and practices suited to Video Learning are addressed in Part 3.

In addition to these learning advantages, Video Learning offers organizations the opportunity to generate new revenues and effect cost savings and efficiencies. These benefits can be realized in several ways. Part 2 of this book cites examples of organizations that are able to:

1. improve training by offering courses that learners can access cost-effectively because they do not have to travel
2. enhance employability by offering degrees or certificate-level courses to learners in workplaces where job changes and reductions are anticipated, thus minimizing costs and stress for both employers and employees and creating a new market for educational institutions
3. organize remedial programs in a timely fashion by making available scarce experts who "cannot be everywhere at once"
4. minimize costs by sharing facilities and equipment among several partners, or by generating new revenue by offering a videoconference service to others

HOW IS VIDEO LEARNING RELATED TO OTHER LEARNING TECHNOLOGIES?

Video Learning can be used alone or in combination with other technologies, as the examples in Part 2 indicate. Indeed, as more and more technologies are mounted on a common computer platform (have you heard of the term "convergence?"), it will become increasingly artificial to consider any one of them independently from the others, at least from the perspective of technology. From a learning viewpoint, however, there will still be reasons why you will, on occasion, want to use other technologies. A few examples illustrate this point.

1. If learners cannot all be available at the same time for a session and the content to be learned is highly visual, you may have to use technologies such as videotapes or CD-ROMs, which learners can view at their own convenience.
2. If rapid movement needs to be conveyed, high-capacity videoconferencing or broadcast television may be needed, with the videotape as an option if the learners cannot be present at the same time.
3. If a lot of factual material has to be presented, print is the most effective medium. You could use paper or computer-based technologies depending on the resources available to your learners.
4. If skills involving listening are to be taught, audiotapes and audioconferencing will probably be the most appropriate technology.

This book concentrates on how to use Video Learning effectively and will enable you to use it alone or in combination with other technologies. References related to other technologies are provided in the Further Readings section.

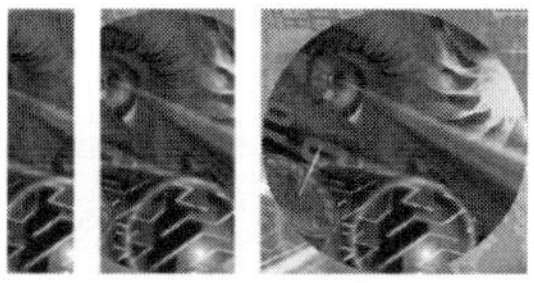

NEEDS ASSESSMENT IS CRITICAL TO ENSURE THAT VIDEO LEARNING IS THE APPROACH THAT BEST ADDRESSES THE NEEDS OF YOUR LEARNERS AND THE CONTENT TO BE LEARNED. THERE IS NOW SUCH A WIDE RANGE OF LEARNING TECHNOLOGIES ON THE MARKET THAT YOU NEED NOT BE "FORCED" TO USE VIDEO LEARNING BECAUSE IT IS THE ONLY MODE AVAILABLE.

IS VIDEO LEARNING EFFECTIVE?

There are a number of misconceptions about Video Learning that users are finding to be just that: misconceptions. We highlight two of the more common inaccurate assertions:

1. The quality of the sound and picture, especially in the more cost-effective two-line mode, is inadequate.
2. Users will not accept constraints such as the amount of preparation required or the difficulty in using the equipment.

Anecdotal data in Part 2 and published reports such as those by Barbara Hakes and her colleagues (1993, 1995) in the United States and Urmil Chugh (1993) at the University of Calgary indicate that such statements are not supported by experience. Learners and instructors in both the public and private sectors report that the picture and sound quality are quite acceptable and that they readily adapted to equipment constraints with practice. Paul Rixon (1996), manager of Videoconferencing Services at the Technical and Further Education Network in South Australia (one of the world's more mature systems) notes:

> Of course, we realize that the images produced by these systems are not of the quality we expect from television, but our users, both students and lecturers, are happy with them, since the quality of the conversation is their measuring stick, not the slickness of the presentation.

That said, it is important that you anticipate and minimize possible resistance. Two strategies are particularly useful in this regard.

1. Be enthusiastic, as positive attitudes are contagious. Starting with a small group of keen supporters will likely generate more momentum than "forcing" a large number of reluctant colleagues to be among the first to try the equipment.
2. At the same time, be realistic about possible downsides. Skeptics are quick to suspect that an unduly optimistic "sales job" is trying to hide serious flaws. Acknowledging that it does take some practice to adjust to Video Learning will be more productive than ignoring the issue.

It is worth repeating that knowing your needs is critical. If you do not need Video Learning, do not insist on using it.

HOW CAN I PERSUADE OTHERS TO TRY VIDEO LEARNING?

Diana Henshaw, director of Continuing Studies at East Carolina University, believes that there are six key strategies that any person or institution should pursue if they want to achieve success in getting colleagues to use Video Learning, or other technologies, to deliver education and training.

1. Consultation: Faculty, technicians and students should be consulted. Support from top administrators is crucial.
2. Goal Setting: Establish realistic goals; consider resources and time lines carefully.
3. Harmony: Ensure that the campus community works together.
4. Milestones: Develop benchmarks of success along the way and celebrate them publicly.
5. Evaluation: Test, evaluate and reengineer on a continuous basis.

6. Application: Apply the lessons learned from every effort to the next learning experiences.

John Mitchell, Australian Video Learning consultant, offered similar advice.

> There are many factors critical to the success of an educational videoconferencing network. Not the least of these is the need to obtain considerable support for the innovation by introducing it in a non-threatening and collaborative manner. Simultaneously, there is a need for thorough project management, providing a framework for roles, responsibilities, help and support.

You might find it useful to draw up a checklist of Diana's suggestions that you can consult regularly if you are involved in planning, implementing and evaluating Video Learning. Even if you do not have a leadership role within your organization, we believe that it will be useful for you to be aware of these strategies.

HOW MUCH DOES VIDEO LEARNING COST?

Users find Video Learning to be cost-efficient, although costs are often context-specific. Nonetheless, since cost savings can be a factor in the decision to use Video Learning, we cite a few generic examples here.

Users in the private sector report significant cost savings because:

1. travel and accommodation expenses are not incurred
2. wages are not "lost" since instructors and learners no longer travel and thus continue to perform their regular duties

Employers are finding that, without the flexible scheduling that Video Learning facilitates, staff would not be able to attend a three-day workshop that required freeing up a minimum of three work days plus travel time. Some employers are willing to pay a higher daily fee for a Video Learning course than for a classroom course because of the improved access and cost savings they can achieve.

Cost is comparative, however. While Video Learning may be less expensive than travel, it may be more expensive than other technologies. Audio Learning, for example, requires only one ordinary telephone line, not the minimum two digital lines that Video Learning needs. Public sector users often have to approach cost from this perspective since their use of technology is generally justified in terms of enhanced learner access to learning resources and equity of opportunity rather than travel or wage savings. Bill Weimer, a consultant from North Carolina, feels that it is becoming feasible to make the business case on grounds other than access: "Videoconferencing, like other technologies, has often been viewed by schools as an additional expense. However, many American policymakers are now wondering whether the use of videoconferencing in schools can lead to cost savings or generate revenues."

We present a template for developing your own business case for videoconferencing in Chapter 3.

CONCLUSION

Now that you have finished reading this chapter, you may begin to realize the opportunity that Video Learning offers, when and why to use it, its relationship to other technologies, common misconceptions and strategies for successful implementation. You have also briefly considered the issue of cost. Now let's learn how Video Learning equipment works.

References

Biner, P. M., Welsh, K. D., Barone, N. M., Summers, M., & Dean, R. S. (1997). The impact of remote-site group size on student satisfaction and relative performance in interactive telecourses. *The American Journal of Distance Education*, *11*(1), 23-33.

Chugh, U. (1993). *Evaluation of a graduate videoconferencing course: Students' and instructors' perspective*. Calgary, AB: University of Calgary, Distance Learning.

Hakes, B., Couchenour, J., Rezabek, L., & Sachs, S. (1995). *Compressed video for instruction: Operations and applications*. Revised and enlarged. Washington, DC: The Association for Educational Communications and Technology.

Hakes, B. T., Sachs, S. G., Box, J., & Couchenour, J. (1993). *Compressed video: Operations and applications*. Washington, DC: The Association for Educational Communications and Technology.

Transport Canada, Training Directorate. (1993, October). *Videoconferencing technology as a medium for distance learning*. Ottawa, ON: Author.

Westbrook, T. S. (1997). Changes in students' attitudes toward graduate business instruction via interactive television. *The American Journal of Distance Education*, *11*(1), 55-69.

Chapter 2

How Does Video Learning Equipment Work?

The second day was much easier than the first, and, by the third day, I don't think that I would have noticed that the classroom was "electronic."

SANDRA HODDER,
SHERIDAN COLLEGE & ONTARIO LEARNING AND TECHNOLOGY EXCHANGE CONSORTIUM (OLTEC),
TORONTO, ONTARIO

INTRODUCTION

This chapter will introduce videoconferencing equipment in jargon-free language. When you have finished reading it, you will know what equipment is required in the classroom, how to link the equipment and how to use it. We recommend that you view the videotape that accompanies this book at some point before, during or after reading this chapter as it contains a section designed to supplement this chapter.

WHAT IS COMPRESSION?

Compressed videoconferencing is a method of communication that can transmit images and sounds directly between classrooms or seminar locations. This technology

1. transmits images, voice and data by converting a television image to a digital signal
2. is interactive, and permits two (point-to-point) or several (multipoint) locations to communicate in real-time
3. is typically transmitted over digital communication lines

The communication lines are often dial-up digital telephone lines. While different from the voice (analog) lines that we use for conversations, these lines are also provided by telephone companies. In some jurisdictions, cable companies offer an equivalent service. For convenience, we refer to the "telephone" lines involved because they tend to be more commonly used by practitioners at this time, and the concept of "number of lines" is easy to understand. However, it is important for you to realize that cable companies and other vendors can also provide the communications service you need. Your technicians can therefore choose different technological solutions to provide the same level of service to your classrooms.

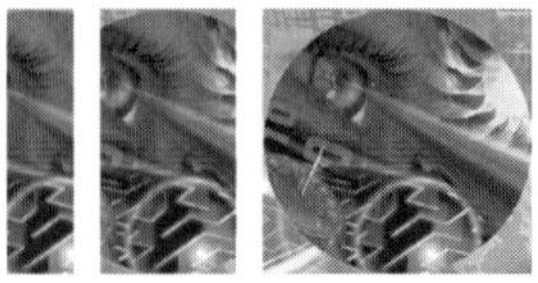

NOT ALL SITES HAVE THE CORRECT TYPE OF DIGITAL SERVICE. IF THIS IS YOUR FIRST TIME USING VIDEO LEARNING, EITHER YOU OR A COLLEAGUE WITH TECHNICAL EXPERTISE SHOULD VERIFY THE KIND OF DIGITAL SERVICE AVAILABLE AT EACH PARTICIPATING SITE BEFORE COMMITTING TO A PROJECT.

WHAT EQUIPMENT WILL BE IN THE ROOM?

At a minimum, users at each site will see:

- one camera
- one television monitor
- one microphone
- a control tablet
- various cords to connect the equipment
- a conventional power cord and power outlet
- two telephone cables and two telephone jacks

As shown in Figure 2.1, vendors generally mount the camera, monitor and microphone on a portable cart and place the control tablet on a table or desk.

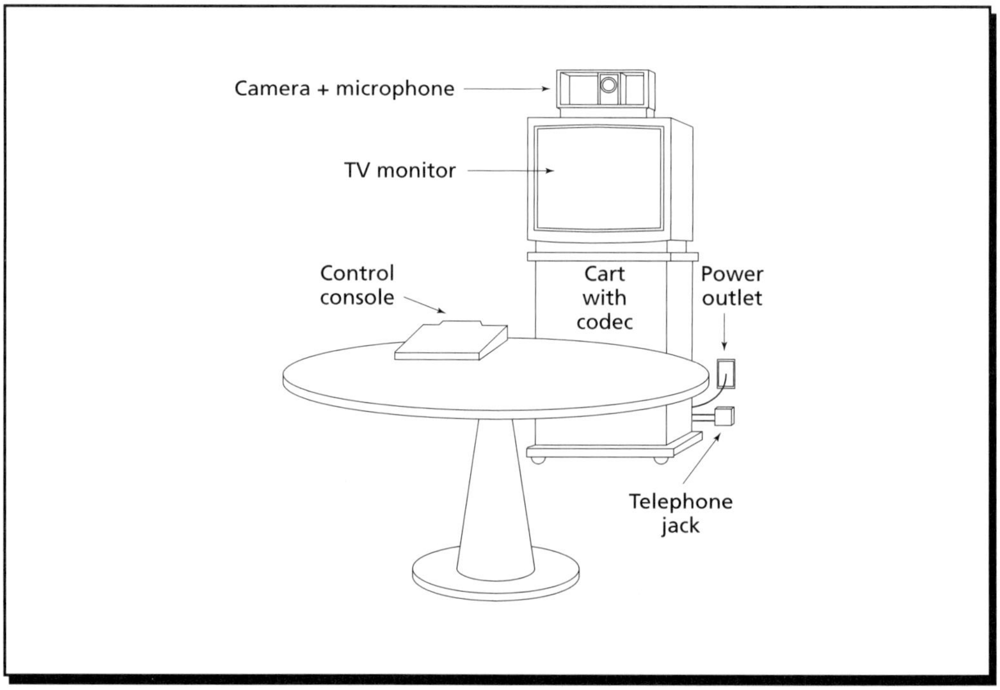

FIGURE 2.1: Example of a basic videoconference system

In addition, an encoder/decoder (codec) is required. Users do not generally see this device as it is stored in the cart. The codec converts the television signal into digital form at the transmitting end (it encodes the signal) and then reconverts the digital signal to a television picture at the receiving end (it decodes the signal). Software in the codec can be proprietary and/or standards-based; we'll describe the difference later in this chapter. The equipment in the cart must be connected to a standard electrical power outlet and to a minimum of two digital communication lines.

Systems can be more complex, as the Franco-Ontarian Distance Education Network demonstrates.

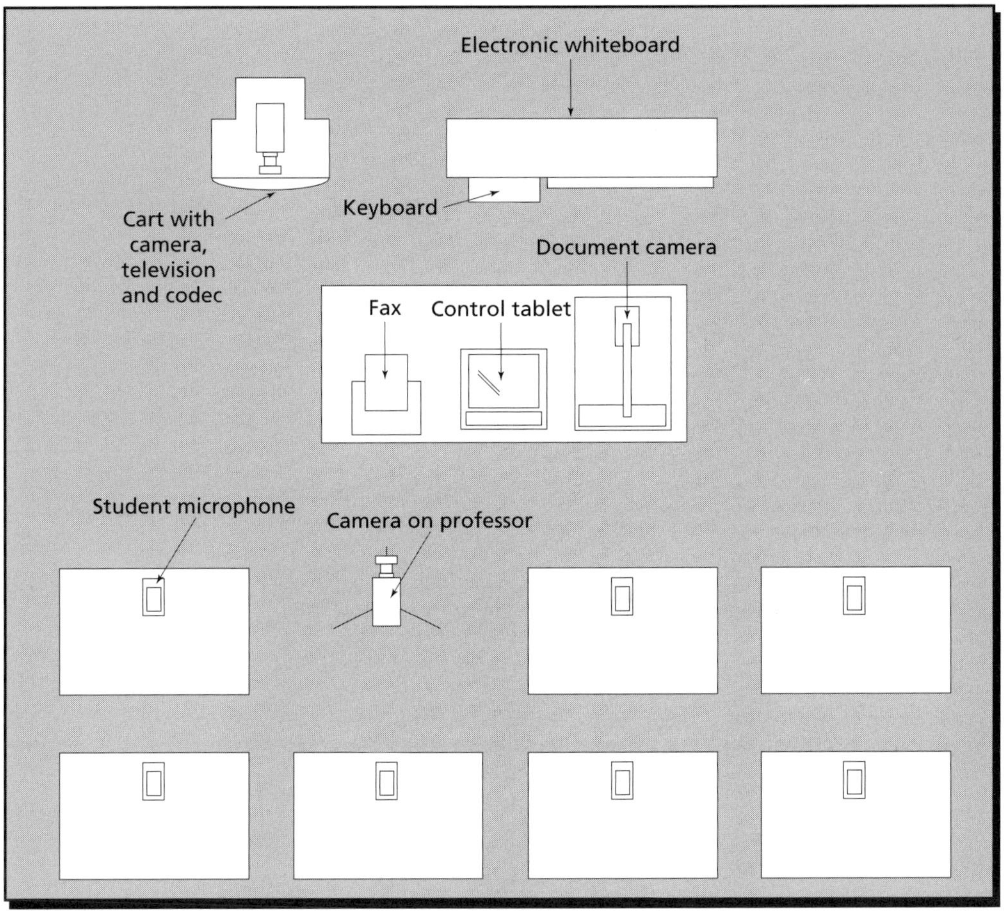

FIGURE 2.2: Example of a room in the Franco-Ontarian Distance Education Network
Source: Lamy, 1995.

As shown in Figure 2.2, each classroom in the Network has:

1. two room cameras (one showing the instructor and one showing the participants)
2. one television monitor
3. a document camera
4. a control tablet
5. an electronic whiteboard (Anything written on this board appears on the boards at the other sites, from which participants can also transmit.)
6. microphones on each student's desk
7. a codec
8. a fax machine

Another common option is a seminar-room configuration that uses a mobile cart and a computer graphics feature instead of the whiteboard (see Figure 2.3).

Careful planning, consideration of your own needs and discussions with other users will enable you to select the layout suitable to your requirements.

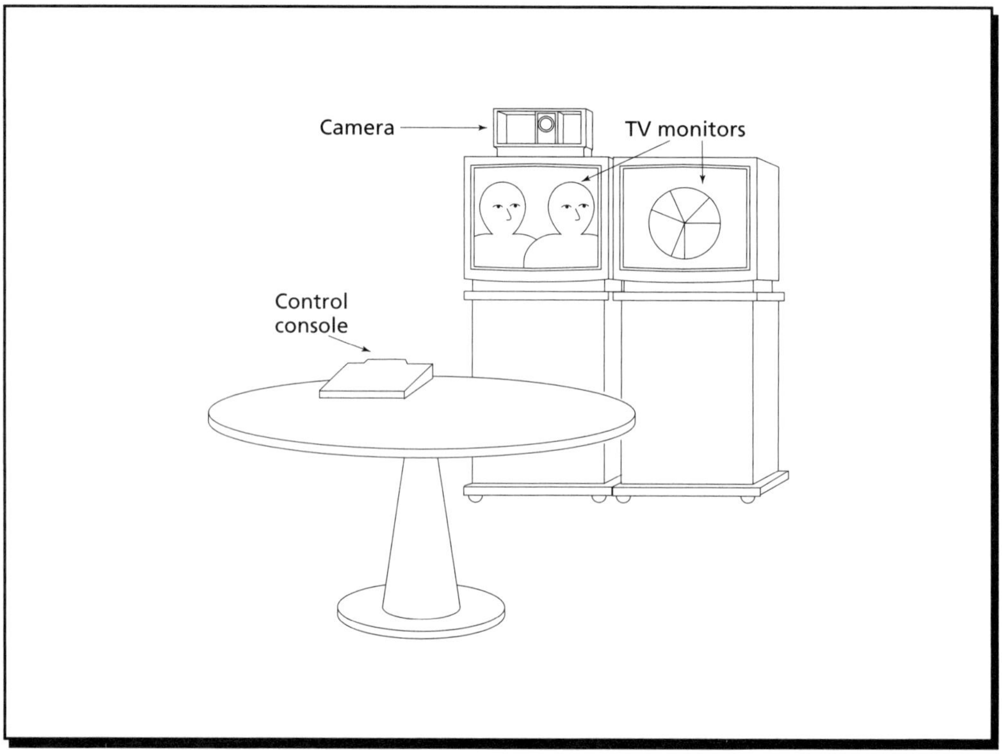

FIGURE 2.3: Example of a videoconference seminar room

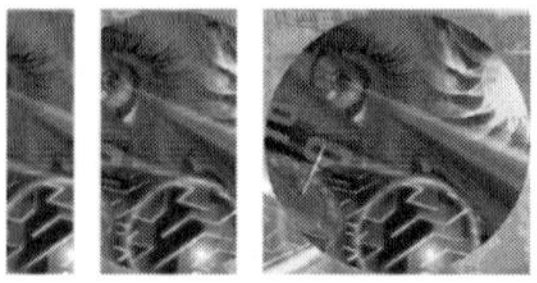

WIRELESS TABLETS MAY BE MORE CONVENIENT TO USE THAN THE MODELS SHOWN IN FIGURES 2.4 TO 2.7.

WHAT DO CONTROL TABLETS LOOK LIKE?

The design of control tablets varies considerably among vendors. Instructor and student reactions to different types of tablets is a critical issue to assess when selecting from different equipment. The VTEL equipment used by Laurentian University (see Figure 2.4), for example, is quite different from the Tandberg equipment used at Northland Pioneer college (see Figure 2.5).

Not only do different vendors offer different tablets, but a single vendor may offer more than one option. Figures 2.6 and 2.7 show two quite distinct control systems offered by PictureTel's Canadian distributor, ADCOM Inc.

We recommend that instructors and learners try using the control tablets before a final selection is made.

HOW ARE SEVERAL ROOMS LINKED TOGETHER?

If two sites want to communicate (point-to-point), one location directly calls the other.

The process of establishing the link is as simple as placing an ordinary telephone call. The sites linked could be two classrooms or two seminar rooms. The number of people in the rooms could vary. For example, a classroom with 20 learners could be linked to a room with one instructor, or a seminar room with five learners could be linked to a classroom with 10 learners and an instructor.

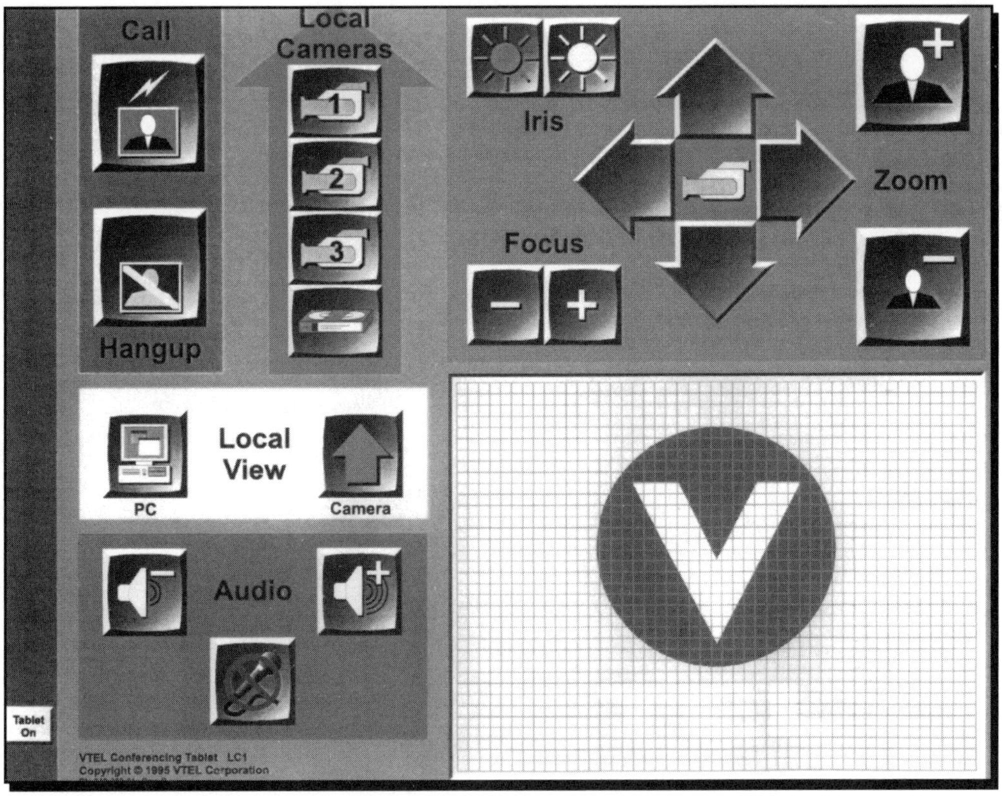

FIGURE 2.4: VTEL control tablet used by Laurentian University in the Franco-Ontarian Distance Education Network. Reprinted with permission of VTEL Corporation.

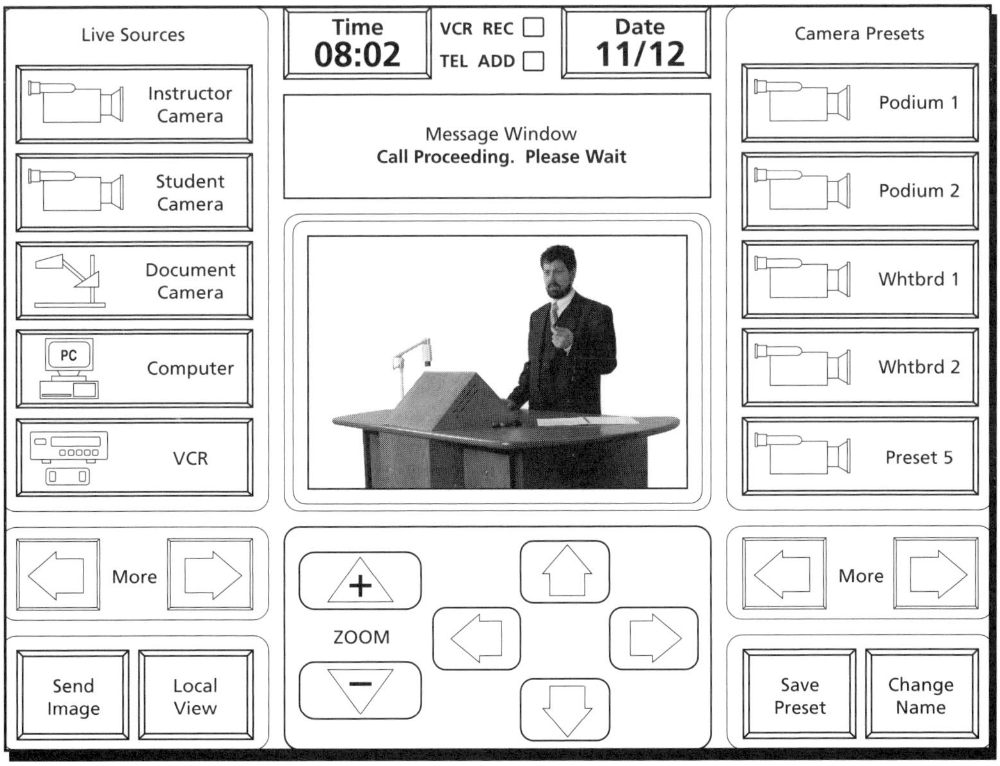

FIGURE 2.5: Tandberg Touch Panel Control used by Northland Pioneer College Reprinted with permission of Tandberg Canada Inc.

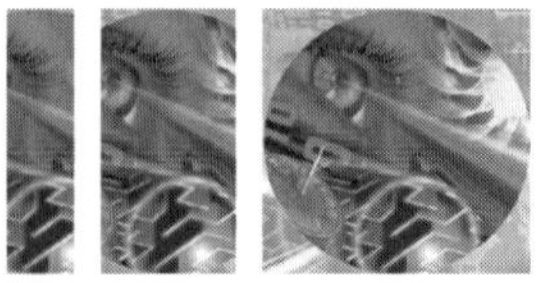

VIDEOCONFERENCING EQUIPMENT IS INCREASINGLY RELIABLE, BUT NOT PERFECT. YOU WILL LOWER YOUR STRESS LEVEL BY PLANNING FOR CONTINGENCIES. HERE'S AN IDEA FROM TRANSPORT CANADA'S EXPERIENCE: VIDEOTAPE YOUR SESSIONS SO THAT IF ANY SITE EXPERIENCES TECHNICAL PROBLEMS, PARTICIPANTS CAN AT LEAST WATCH THE TAPE AT A LATER DATE.

If three or more sites are involved (multipoint), all sites call a device called a bridge, which links them so that they can all see and hear one another (see Figure 2.8).

Regardless of whether 2 or 20 sites are linked, the technical configuration is called a videoconference.

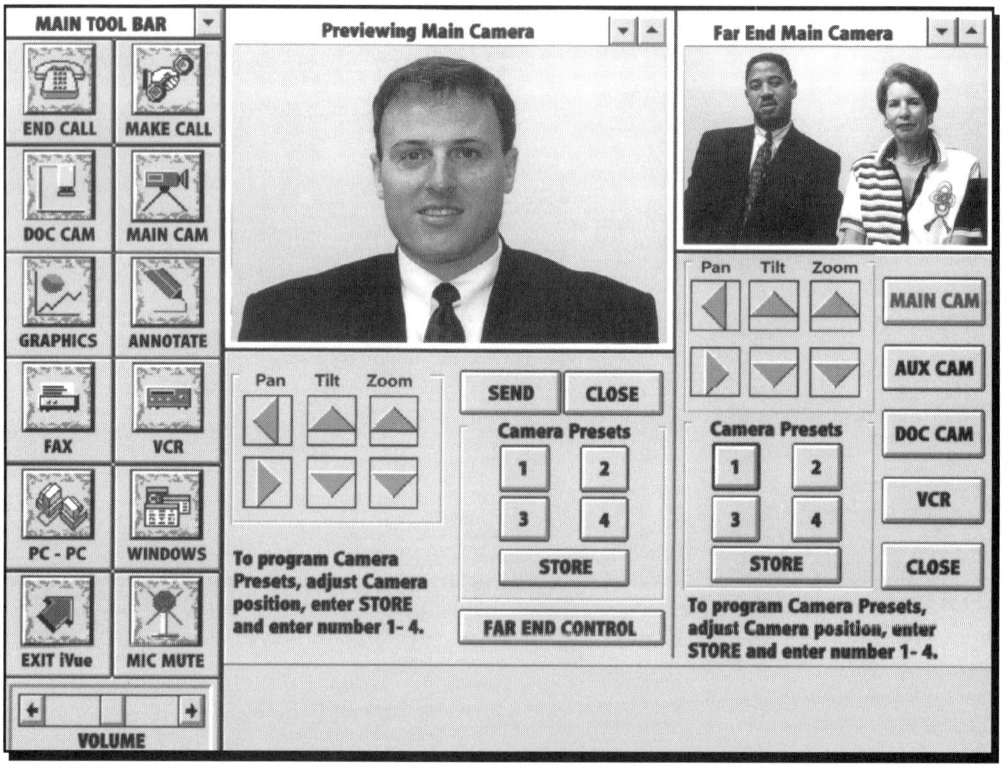

FIGURE 2.6: PictureTel control tablet used by OLTEC
Reprinted with permission of ADCOM Inc.

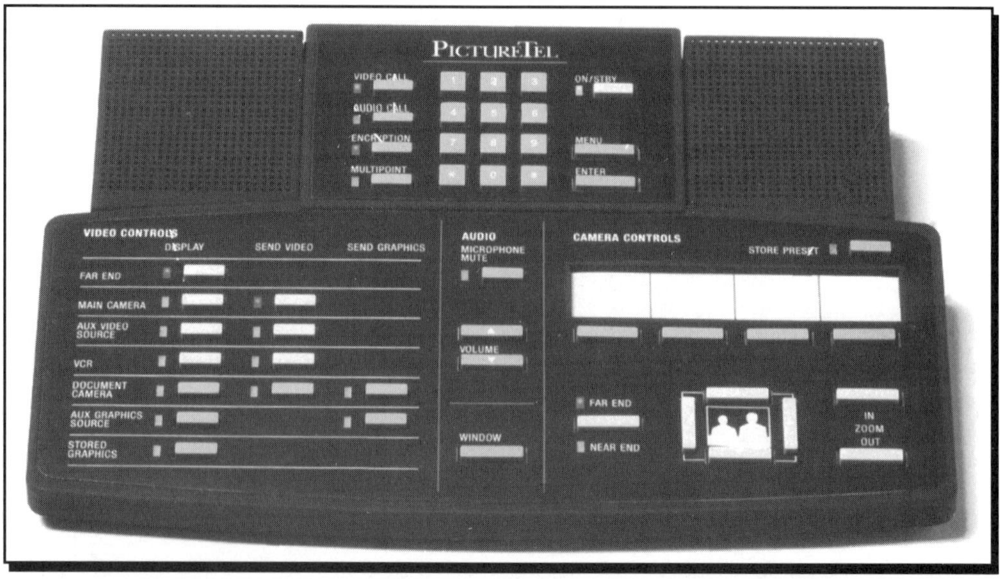

FIGURE 2.7: PictureTel control tablet used by Huron County Board of Education
Reprinted with permission of PictureTel Corporation.

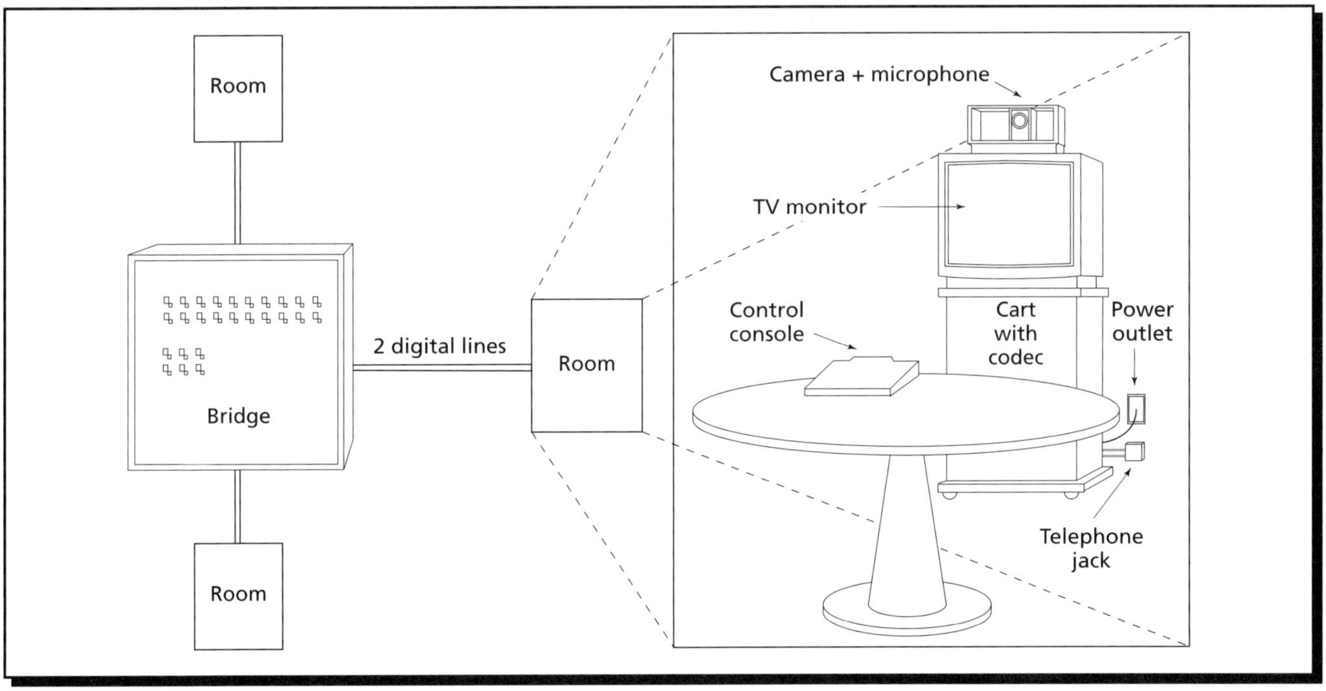

FIGURE 2.8: Multipoint videoconferencing

WHAT SOFTWARE IS REQUIRED?

As we noted above, one or both of two types of (proprietary) videoconferencing software is contained in the codec: (1) that which is specific to a manufacturer and (2) that which meets an international standard established in 1990 by the International Telegraph and Telephone Consultative Committee (CCITT).

If every site has equipment made by the same manufacturer, and if the "brand name" (proprietary) software is used, then any special features unique to that supplier's equipment can be used. If sites have different brand name equipment with software that meets international standards, the different brands will interconnect and participants at all sites will be able to see and talk to one another. However, when using CCITT software, the ability to use special proprietary features will be limited. Some users feel that picture quality is also affected.

In general, proprietary software enhances the use of manufacturers' special features and options, while standards-based software permits highly flexible basic videoconferencing connections to be made among users. Some vendors are so convinced of the importance of interconnection that they do not have their own separate proprietary software. Their products are solely standards-based.

WHAT IS DESKTOP VIDEOCONFERENCING?

Videoconferencing's backbone is digital, computer-based technology. The codec is, in effect, a highly sophisticated computer. As computer chips become more powerful, they are creating the opportunity to transmit pictures and sounds directly from a personal computer; they are creating desktop videoconferencing. Paul Guild (1993), a professor at the University of Waterloo in

Waterloo, Ontario, is one of Canada's early pioneers in exploring the potential of this technology. He reports: "Interest is growing in using desktop videoconferencing in distance education." His early work is described in a newsletter published by the Centre for System Science at Simon Fraser University in Burnaby, British Columbia, where he is chairperson of Management of Technology, a position held jointly with the University of Waterloo.

Desktop videoconferencing appeals particularly strongly to organizations that:

1. already have a strong computer infrastructure (most of its employees or clients already have computers and modems on their desks)
2. find that one-to-one applications are more efficient than the group-based approach of videoconferencing in the classroom

PRODUCTS ARE BEING DEVELOPED SO QUICKLY THAT OBSOLESCENCE AND CONFUSION ARE SERIOUS CONCERNS. OUR ADVICE IS TO THINK STRATEGICALLY AND BE HIGHLY FLEXIBLE IF YOU PLAN TO TRY THIS TECHNOLOGY.

Desktop videoconferencing can function on a computer and one standard, voice-grade (not digital) telephone line. The computer has to be equipped with a modem and one of the many types of software being developed to facilitate desktop videoconferencing. Certain minimum technical capacities must exist in the computer and the modem for the software to function, so you may have to invest some time in understanding the technical terms if you plan to capitalize on this technology.

For example, if you do not need a high degree of resolution (picture quality), there are basic products on the market today, such as Cornell University's CUSeeMe software, that may suit your needs and are available at no cost through the Internet. If you want a higher quality, however, you may wish to conduct pilot projects that test a range of products until you find one that meets your needs and seems stable enough to warrant a large-scale purchase. Leigh Anne Rettinger, a graduate student at North Carolina State University, produced an index designed to aid in comparing the many desktop videoconferencing systems that are being produced as part of her master's thesis. (An electronic address for the thesis is given in the References section at the end of this chapter.) We describe a case study in desktop videoconferencing at East Carolina University and a case study in the use of desktop videoconferencing for special needs students in Chapter 4.

ONE OF THE FORCES DRIVING THE DEVELOPMENT OF COST-EFFECTIVE, HIGH-QUALITY DESKTOP VIDEOCONFERENCING PRODUCTS IS THE TREND FOR COMPANIES TO ALLOW EMPLOYEES TO WORK IN THEIR HOMES, ALSO CALLED TELECOMMUTING. THE UNITED STATES TELECOMMUTING ADVISORY COUNCIL ESTIMATES THAT BY THE YEAR 2000, 25 MILLION PEOPLE WILL TELECOMMUTE.

Desktop videoconferencing is a rapidly developing technology. Keep it in mind when you purchase your next computer!

CONCLUSION

In this chapter you have learned the basics of videoconferencing technology. Let's now consider the technical and human facilities you will require to use this equipment effectively as a learning tool.

References

Lamy, T. (1995). *Videocommunication: A faculty guide to learning and communicating by compressed videoconferencing* (J. Roberts, Trans.). Sudbury, ON: Laurentian University: Centre for Continuing Education.

Rettinger, L. A. (n.d.). *Desktop videoconferencing: Technology and use for remote seminar delivery*. Unpublished Master's thesis, North Carolina University. Available at <http://www2.ncsu.edu/eos/service/ece/project/succeed_info/larettin/thesis/>

Shell, B. (1993, March). The virtual classroom. *Update, 5*(2). Burnaby, BC: Simon Fraser University, Centre for System Science.

Chapter 3

What Resources Will I Need?

We tried to get a concrete sense of what a videoconferencing project would entail at a very early stage in our planning. I am a "hands-on" learner and prefer to see concrete examples rather than read about them. So, before we made any decisions, we visited suppliers so that we could actually try the equipment and we met with other users to get their advice on what to do.

JOE GAMBINO,
ONTARIO REAL ESTATE ASSOCIATION,
DON MILLS, ONTARIO

INTRODUCTION

OTHER HUMAN RESOURCE ISSUES RELATED TO LEARNING DESIGN AND EVALUATION SUPPORT ARE COVERED IN PART 3.

Some minimum communication, space, human and financial resources are required for Video Learning. In this chapter you will review communication, room design and technical personnel requirements. You can then learn how to develop a business plan that incorporates the key cost issues and addresses the challenge of obsolescence. We believe that you need to appreciate these issues in a general way in order to understand the context that will shape some of your learning design choices.

WHAT COMMUNICATION FACILITIES WILL I NEED?

We address three aspects of this topic: (1) the range of choices available to your institution, (2) the clarity of picture you require and (3) one way to minimize the cost of high-quality pictures.

Choices Available to Your Institution

REMEMBER THAT THE DIGITAL SERVICE REQUIRED FOR VIDEOCONFERENCING CAN BE PROVIDED, IN SOME JURISDICTIONS, BY VENDORS SUCH AS CABLE COMPANIES.

The ways in which your institution can acquire the digital service needed to transmit videoconferencing signals is regulated by agencies such as the Canadian Radio-television and Telecommunications Commission in Canada or the Federal Communications Commission in the United States. Alternatively, as in Australia, governments may control communications policies directly. These regulations and government legislation will significantly affect how much you pay and what vendors you will deal with.

"The problem is not the technology, it's the regulations," suggests Bob Clark, University College of the Cariboo in British Columbia. Participants in a CompuServe discussion group agree. George Gilder, a U.S.-based critic of the telecommunications industry, noted that "the problem is the regulatory environment that prevents telephone companies from laying fiber to homes."

Considering Picture Quality

A compressed video signal requires a minimum of two digital telephone lines. The quality of the picture is affected by the number of telephone lines used: the greater the compression (the fewer telephone lines used), the poorer the image quality. In particular, participants' movements can become broken and fuzzy. In selecting the number of lines to be used, the content of the application becomes important as the need for clear resolution has to be balanced against the higher capital and operating costs of more lines.

This book refers to the use of either two or six telephone lines. However, vendor materials and other literature often refer to 112 or 128 Kbps, or kilobits per second (our two-line mode), and 384 or 336 Kbps (our six-line mode). You may want to become familiar with this technical terminology if you live in a jurisdiction where cable companies can readily provide service to your institution or if you prefer to deal in data speed measurements. However, non-technically minded users need only appreciate that there is a difference in quality and cost depending on whether two or six lines are used.

MOST USERS CONSIDER THAT FOUR LINES IS NOT A RELEVANT COMPROMISE, AND THAT THE CRITICAL CHOICE IS BETWEEN TWO OR SIX LINES.

Minimizing Cost

If you plan to use Video Learning for a wide variety of applications, only some of which require six-line quality, you may want to install six telephone lines and a "black box," which will enable you to vary the number of lines you use in a particular session. Such a strategy will not reduce the capital cost of the six lines, but it will reduce your long-distance costs and result in operating cost savings.

HOW SHOULD THE ROOM BE LAID OUT?

As we noted in Chapter 2, videoconferencing equipment configurations can vary. However, the minimum room requirements are constant: (1) a power outlet adjacent to where the telephone lines are installed and (2) classroom or seminar room furniture.

The room's light and acoustical characteristics are critical. Lighting should be tested, as low levels of lighting will adversely affect picture quality, making it hard to distinguish people's features. On the other hand, bright light from overhead fluorescent fixtures or windows can reflect off television monitors, making viewing difficult. Lighting levels should be adjusted to an appropriate level. If possible, the room should be carpeted, and drapes, or some other sound-absorbing material, should cover the windows. If there are no windows in the room, fabric or some other treatment should be installed on at least one of the walls.

Once these features have been dealt with, the room can be designed in a number of different ways, as Figures 3.1 and 3.2 illustrate. Other examples of room layouts are provided in Chapter 4.

Another decision to be made is whether you want to dedicate one room for videoconferencing applications or use several rooms. If only one room is used, decide whether the equipment should be permanently installed there and whether security will be a problem. Can you keep the room locked when it is

VENDORS GENERALLY PROVIDE EXCELLENT ADVICE, BUT YOU SHOULD ALSO CONSIDER VISITING OTHER USERS TO SEE THEIR SITES IN OPERATION. THEY MAY HAVE FOUND COST-EFFECTIVE WAYS TO ACCOMPLISH GOALS SIMILAR TO YOURS. THEIR EXPERIENCE MAY BE HELPFUL TO YOU IN OTHER WAYS.

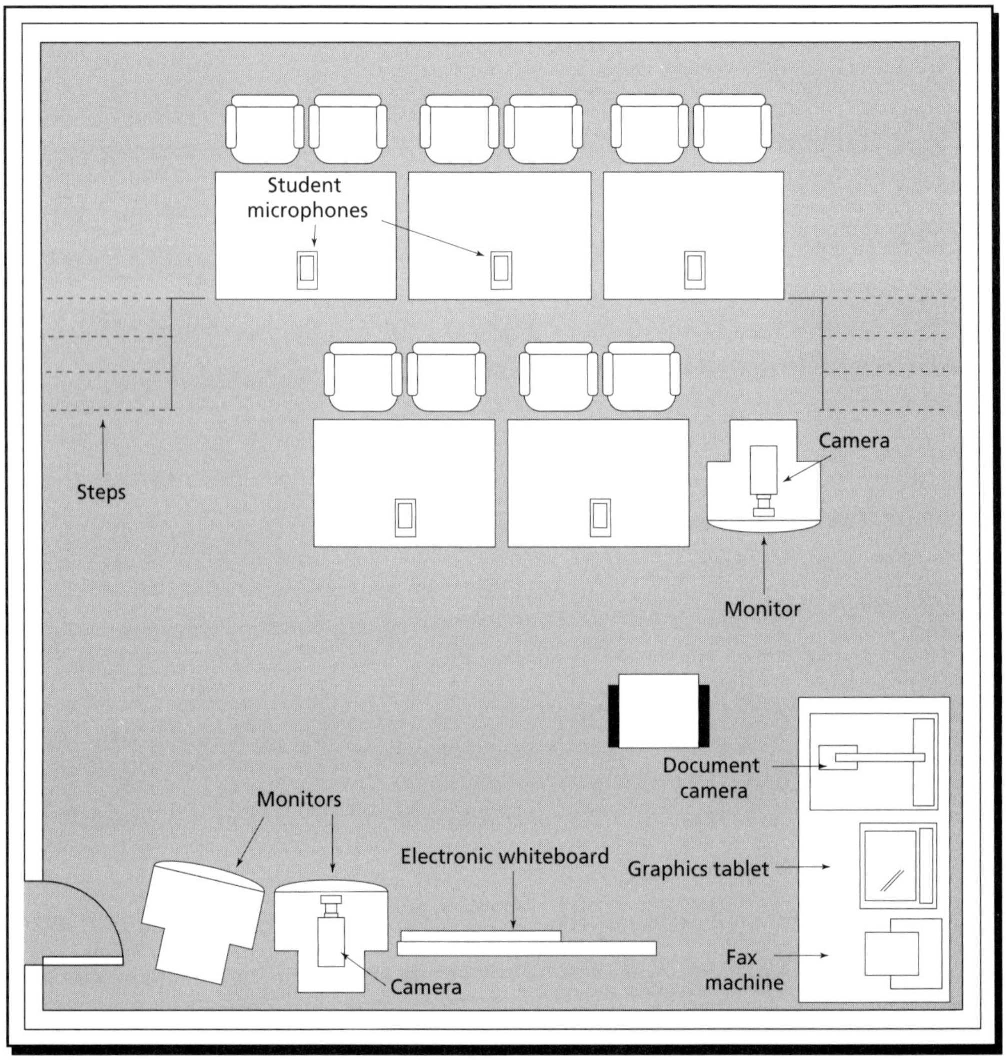

FIGURE 3.1: Example of a tiered classroom design

not in use? Will access to keys to the room be an issue? If the room is used for other purposes, should lockable storage facilities be installed in the room, or will the equipment be brought to the room on a demand basis? If the equipment is to be moved from room to room, your audio-visual service could move the cart around on demand just as they move slide projectors and VCR units. However, digital telephone lines, power plugs, draperies and other facilities should be installed in each room that you plan to use.

WHAT TECHNICAL PERSONNEL ARE NEEDED?

Technical personnel generally perform three types of functions: (1) setting up, operating and troubleshooting the equipment, (2) training users and (3) maintenance. We will deal with the first two functions in this section and consider the third when we develop the business case.

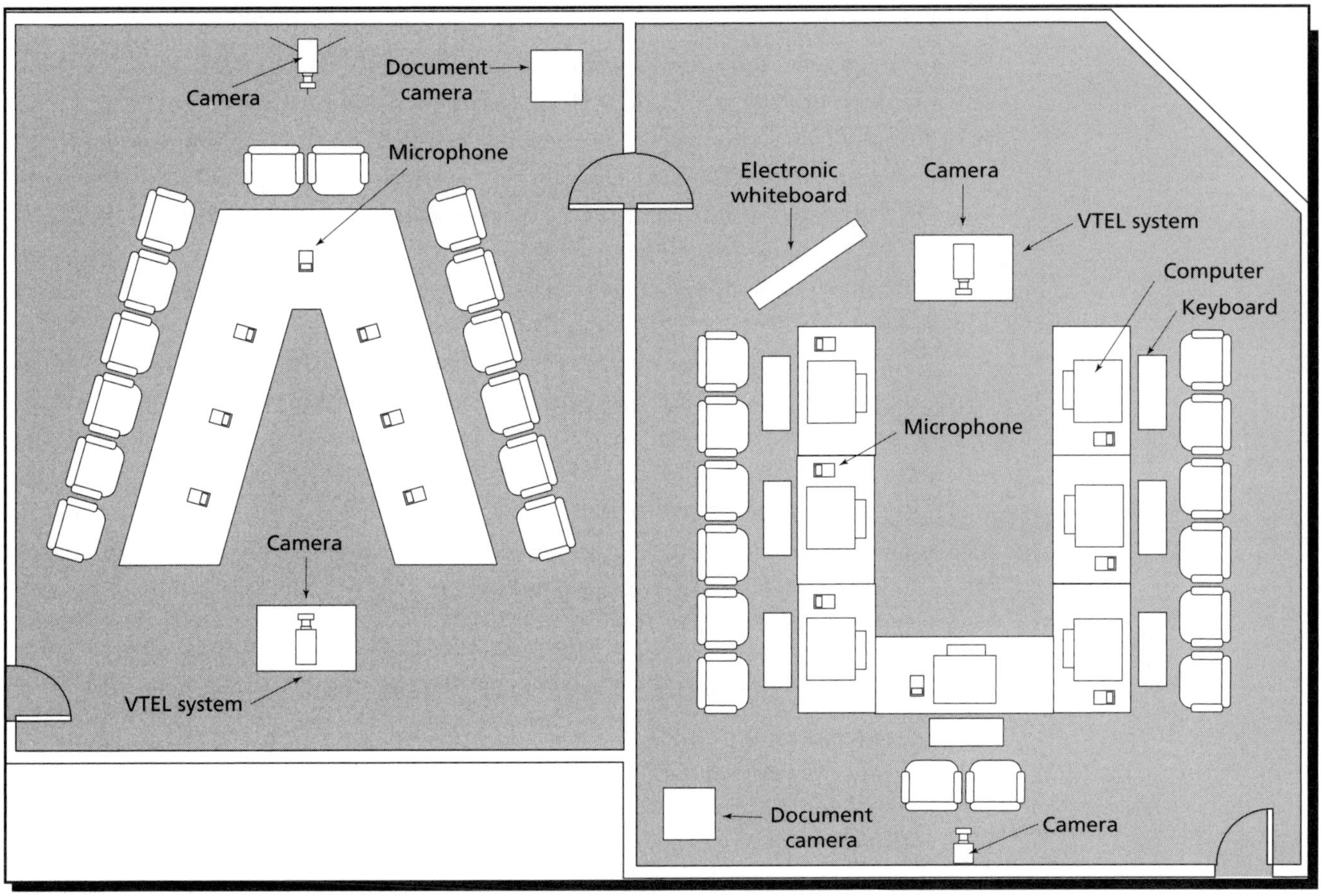

FIGURE 3.2: Examples of classroom designs at Le Collège des Grands Lacs, Toronto, Ontario

Equipment Setup, Operation and Troubleshooting

It is a good idea to have someone designated at each site to be responsible for setting up, operating and troubleshooting the equipment. There are many ways to do this, some of which depend on the length of your learning event.

Many institutions find that a student in a 10- to 12-week course can assume the task at each site with a minimum degree of training. In a three-month course, however, the instructor and other learners may become quite familiar with operating the equipment and will depend less and less on a student operator.

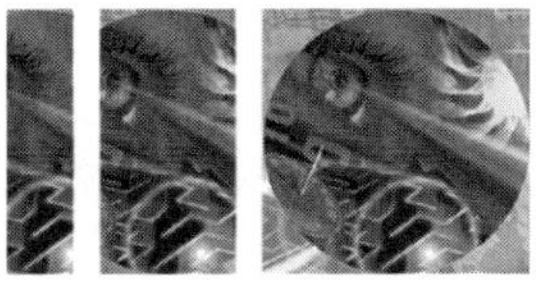

AN IDEA FROM DENIS MAYER, LAURENTIAN UNIVERSITY, SUDBURY, ONTARIO: HAVE A TECHNICIAN ON CALL WHO CAN BE REACHED AT ANY TIME DURING A COURSE SESSION THROUGH A PAGER OR CELL PHONE.

The degree of support the student operator requires from a trained technician depends on your situation. It is generally a good idea to plan for a high level of support at the beginning of a learning event. Typically, student operators become more and more adept at troubleshooting the equipment and require less and less support from a technician.

On the other hand, brief training events require in-house or external technical support to be continuously present at each site throughout the event. Short sessions prevent users from learning much about how to use the equipment. A technician should therefore perform all equipment operations, especially if the instructor is external to the organization and is paid by the hour.

User Training

Regardless of the length of a session, the instructor and participants should all learn how to use the equipment (for example, which buttons to press) and what functionalities it possesses. Doing so demystifies the technology and also enables both instructor and learners to use it in ways that are appropriate to their learning goals. For example, learners taking a course in interviewing techniques might need the close-up function to catch details of facial expression, while learners in a physiotherapy course would be more interested in taking longer shots so they can see overall body movement.

Training can be acquired from your vendor at the time of purchase, as can some degree of troubleshooting and maintenance. Since vendors usually charge for support after the initial installation, it is important that your organization calculate and compare the cost of purchasing vendor support with the expense of hiring your own person on a full- or part-time basis. Even if you choose to contract with a vendor, it is a good idea to have at least one person on staff or on contract who is knowledgeable about the technology and who can supplement vendor training and technical support.

WHAT IS THE BUSINESS CASE FOR VIDEO LEARNING?

Now that we have highlighted generic communication, room layout and technical personnel requirements, let's examine three categories of cost that you need to consider when developing your own, context-specific business case: (1) your own internal costs, (2) the capital and operating costs of videoconferencing equipment if you purchase it and (3) the operating costs if you use publicly available rooms. Then, let's ask "whose cost?"

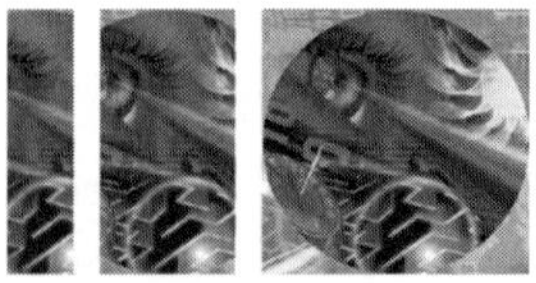

REMEMBER TO CONSIDER DIRECT AND INDIRECT COSTS, AS WELL AS COST AVOIDANCE AND REPLACEMENT ISSUES.

Your Own Internal Costs

Depending on the policies within your organization, you may have to allocate costs such as the instructor's wages, the participants' time, classroom rental, photocopying, meals and incidentals to the videoconference. Participant time in the private sector may represent employee wages if the training takes place during paid working hours. In the public sector, learner time is often not valued since, for example, the time of grade 10 students has no economic value.

Such costs are relevant whether you purchase your own equipment or rent facilities from someone else.

Purchasing Your Own Equipment

Since prices are constantly changing, we present an analysis of the categories you should use when talking to various vendors, rather than specific prices. It is important that you obtain information for each item shown in Table 3.1.

The capital cost categories consist of

1. the basic system offered by the vendor—generally a variation on the equipment shown in Figure 2.1

TABLE 3.1: CAPITAL COSTS OF ACQUIRING VIDEOCONFERENCING EQUIPMENT

FEATURE	VENDOR A	VENDOR B	VENDOR C
Basic system			
Option package			
Installation charge			
Service contract			
Training			
Total			

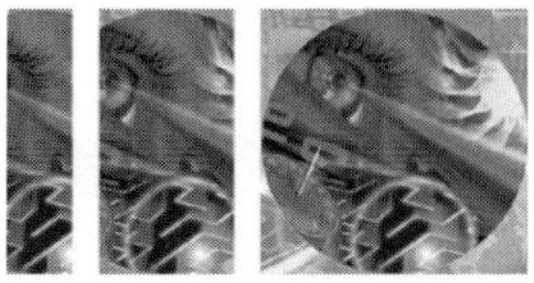

IF YOU DO NOT WANT TO INCUR CAPITAL COSTS FOR A PILOT PROJECT, INVESTIGATE THE AVAILABILITY OF FULLY EQUIPPED ROOMS PROVIDED, USUALLY AT AN HOURLY RATE, BY PRIVATE SECTOR VENDORS AND BY PUBLIC SECTOR CONSORTIA.

2. the option package that best meets your needs (Options can range from an extra camera to graphics interfaces with computer devices.)
3. the installation charge made by the equipment vendor
4. the service contract offered by the vendor if you intend to purchase it in advance as a capital cost item
5. charges for training offered by the vendor (Most provide a basic level of training at no charge, with an option for additional training for a fee.)

The issue of a service contract needs to be carefully considered. For example, you can purchase the contract on a long-term basis (usually three years) as a capital item, or on an annual basis as an operating expense. There is usually a slight saving in the vendor's price if the capital option is taken. Your institution's purchasing department may have policies that affect your decision. Another factor is whether you will engage your own technician on a part- or full-time basis to service the equipment, in which case a service contract is probably not needed.

In addition to the vendor's capital costs, the telephone company or other service provider normally charges a one-time-only cost to install the service they provide at your site. Be sure to include this charge in your capital budget once you have selected your equipment vendor. In general, this cost varies according to the number of lines you need, not the equipment you select. The minimum they have to provide to make the equipment functional is two digital telephone lines and a special electronics package. Other more sophisticated installations may be required depending on your application.

Aside from your own internal operating costs and the issue of a service contract (or a technician's salary or support), the other major operating cost is

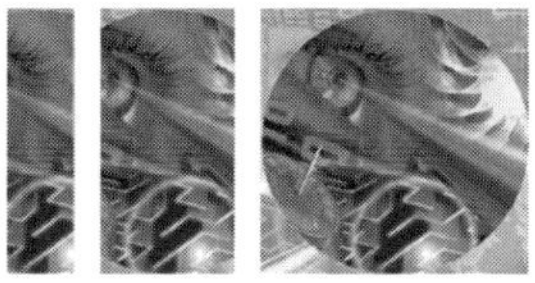

BE SURE THAT YOUR TELEPHONE COMPANY, OR OTHER APPROPRIATE VENDOR, CAN PROVIDE THE DIGITAL LINES. AS STEPHEN OLIVER FOUND OUT IN HURON COUNTY, YOUR BUSINESS PLAN MAY HAVE TO ACCOMMODATE DELAYS IF DIGITAL SERVICE IS NOT YET IN PLACE IN YOUR AREA. YOU MAY NEED, FOR EXAMPLE, TO ASK THE EQUIPMENT VENDOR TO EXTEND THE VALIDITY OF THE QUOTED PRICE IF THE COMMUNICATION SERVICE IS NOT READILY AVAILABLE.

TABLE 3.2: CALCULATING THE COMMUNICATION COMPONENT OF OPERATING COSTS

TYPE OF SERVICE	MONTHLY SERVICE CHARGE	LONG-DISTANCE		BRIDGE CHARGE
		PRIME	DISCOUNT	
Two-line mode				
Six–line mode				

communication charges. A template for calculating these costs based on the telephone company model is provided in Table 3.2.

Each of these charges can be summarized as follows, depending on the type of service (the number of lines or degree of resolution) you decide to purchase from the telephone company. The two-line and six-line modes are provided in Table 3.2 for illustrative purposes only.

1. A fixed monthly service charge will cover the cost of being connected; the principle is the same as paying the service portion of your monthly telephone bill.
2. Long-distance charges will be incurred each time you link two or more sites outside your local calling area. The cost will vary depending on the length of your session and on whether a prime, non-discounted rate or reduced rate applies. The discount will depend on factors such as the time of day a call is made or whether a volume discount plan is available at your institution.
3. If three or more sites are linked (see Figure 2.9), a bridge charge will apply. Like long-distance costs, bridge charges will vary depending on the length of your session.

Renting Facilities

As we mentioned in Chapter 1, one technique for reducing costs, especially at the pilot project stage, is to rent rooms that are already fully equipped and staffed.

TABLE 3.3: SAMPLE REQUIREMENTS SHEET
Costs for a [ ] Hour [ ] line Videoconference

SITE	SETUP	RENTAL	LONG DISTANCE	BRIDGE	TAXES	ROOM CAPACITY REQ'D
						[#] people
						[#]
						[#]
						[#]
						[#]
						[#]
TOTAL						N/A

NOTE: Please confirm that rooms **are** available on the following dates and times.
Thursday, May 29, 199_ , 12 p.m. to 2 p.m. & Friday, May 30, 199_ , 12 p.m. to 2 p.m.

Table 3.3 presents a template you can use when dealing with private or public sector colleagues when determining how much it would cost to rent their facilities.

The table consists of the following categories:

1. the sites where learners and instructor are located
2. the room setup charge, if any
3. the hourly rental rate for the room
4. the long-distance charges involved
5. the bridge charge if three or more sites are involved
6. any relevant taxes
7. the room capacity that you need

Some organizations include user orientation in their setup charge and have someone on call for technical emergencies as part of that fee. Room capacity and room layout are important: you don't want to have three people "lost" in a tiered room set up for 50 people, nor do you want to have 30 people squashed into a room designed to hold 10 people.

Whose Cost?

Organizations find that the business case that results from analyzing these costs can vary depending on whose perspective is adopted. Joe Gambino of the Ontario Real Estate Association's Education Department, reports that:

> the business case for Video Learning rests, for us, on the advantages it offers the learners. Our Association does not save any money using this approach, but learners do. They avoid the travel and accommodation costs of having to come to a central location to take the course. Learners also benefit from the fact that we can offer courses more often now than we did in the past. When we first started offering these short, 40-hour courses in 1989, which are mandatory for relicensing, we would offer them infrequently and required a minimum number of registrants to cover our costs. We often found that we did not have the required minimum when the only way to take the courses was to travel to a central location. Now, with videoconferencing, we can offer courses more often as it is easier to get the minimum number of people since they can be distributed in several locations. Learners may have to pay a slightly higher registration fee for the videoconference courses, but they consider it excellent value for the money since they avoid the inconvenience of course cancellations and the expenses involved in travel.

Other examples of the business case for Video Learning are given in Part 2.

HOW CAN I MINIMIZE THE RISK OF OBSOLESCENCE?

A common question related to the issue of developing a business case for videoconferencing is: "But what's the point of acquiring anything when it will almost immediately become obsolete?"

In spite of what seems to be rapid changes in equipment, there are a number of short-term ways to minimize the risk of obsolescence. They include:

1. lease or rental (not purchase) of equipment that is installed in your premises

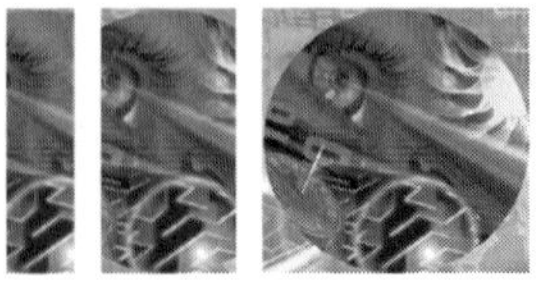

DO NOT WAIT FOR A PERFECT MATCH BETWEEN TECHNOLOGY AND NEED; INFORMATION TECHNOLOGY IS CONSTANTLY EVOLVING WITH NO END IN SIGHT. SENSIBLE COMPROMISE AND NEW APPROACHES TO DELIVERY AND USE ARE REQUIRED FOR PROGRESS. GETTING STARTED EARLY, IN CONCERT WITH FOCUSED EVALUATION, IS A "HIDDEN BENEFIT" IN THIS PROCESS. THE TROUBLE WITH "WAIT AND SEE" IS THAT IT CAN BECOME "WAIT AND LOSE." (DAVID SADLEIR, OLTEC TECHNOLOGY COMMITTEE AND PROFESSOR OF INDUSTRIAL ENGINEERING AT THE UNIVERSITY OF TORONTO, TORONTO, ONTARIO)

2. rental of facilities in rooms managed by organizations such as vendors, consortia mandated to serve public and/or private sector clients, or organizations seeking extra revenue by renting their equipment when they are not using it
3. negotiating cost-effective upgrade packages as part of your initial purchase contract
4. purchasing equipment and software that conforms to international standards
5. forming a consortium of users to negotiate cost-effective purchase, lease or upgrade rates and prices based on shared technical plans
6. being practical about and understanding your "real" needs (you probably won't need every upgrade that comes along)

Since change is inevitable, developing appropriate capital reserves is a critical long-term strategy, as is thinking strategically and flexibly rather than focusing on a "carved-in-stone" plan.

CONCLUSION

In this chapter you learned about communication, space and technical personnel issues. We then integrated these factors with the technology options described in Chapter 2 to recommend templates that can contribute to your business planning process. We are now at the end of Part 1.

Part 2 gives a number of examples of how public and private sector organizations are successfully using Video Learning.

PART 2

WHO IS USING COMPRESSED VIDEO LEARNING SUCCESSFULLY?

Chapter 4 gives you the chance to learn from other people's experiences by describing applications drawn from the work of pioneers throughout the world who are developing Compressed Video Learning applications in workplace, school, college and university settings. Models involving consortia, special needs learners and minority cultures are also included in this section. Instructors or project coordinators, contacted by telephone or e-mail share their views on a wide range of issues that need to be considered when you develop a learning design plan appropriate to the needs of the learners you serve.

Chapter 4

How Can I Learn from Other People's Experiences?

In Australia, as in other countries throughout the world, universities, technical colleges, school systems, hospitals, corporations and governments are finding that compressed videoconferencing is a vital tool that is enabling them to better serve learners.

JOHN MITCHELL,
VIDEO LEARNING CONSULTANT,
UNLEY, AUSTRALIA

INTRODUCTION

In this chapter you will have the opportunity to learn from 15 Video Learning experiences drawn from the public and private sectors in North America, Europe and Australia. Before presenting these success stories, we provide a framework for you to use when reading them. The framework consists of (1) the selection factors we used, (2) the way in which information is presented in each story and (3) some themes for you to watch for when reading the balance of the chapter.

WHAT FRAMEWORK SHOULD I APPLY TO THESE SUCCESS STORIES?

Why Were They Chosen?

The projects were chosen to illustrate the rich variety of ways in which Video Learning is used and to outline the factors that instructors thought were critical to facilitate Video Learning successfully.

Applications in the formal education sector range from the secondary school to the postgraduate university level, where both credit and non-credit activities are being developed. Workplace applications range from engineering (OLTEC) and health professionals (Memorial University of Newfoundland, Bell/ARF VideoLink) to banking (CIBC), telecommunications (NBTel) and government (Transport Canada). Cultural minorities (KAYAS Cultural College and Francophone projects) and special needs groups (Cambrian College) find that Video Learning links previously isolated groups of learners.

Many organizations are involved in more than one type of application and are actively seeking partnerships outside their own sector (the Huron County Board of Education) and outside their country (East Carolina University). Learning takes place within different organizational contexts. Some institutions, such as Memorial University of Newfoundland, focus primarily on requirements and partnerships within an existing institution. Others, such as

EuroPACE 2000, employ a consortium approach and create a new organization to serve mutual needs. Different business cases can be developed, depending on existing organizational patterns. For example, Transport Canada estimates that it saves money from its own budget, while the Addiction Research Foundation projects that savings will be achieved by its clients, not its staff.

How Is Information about Them Organized?

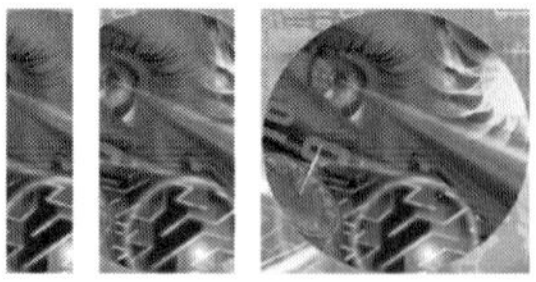

SINCE MANY OF THE PROJECTS INVOLVE VARIOUS TYPES OF CROSS-SECTORAL AND INTERNATIONAL PARTNERSHIPS AND MORE THAN ONE TYPE OF APPLICATION, YOU MIGHT WANT TO SKIM THE CASE STUDIES AND RETURN TO READ IN MORE DETAIL THOSE THAT PARTICULARLY INTEREST YOU.

The case studies are grouped into four categories:

1. Workplace users: CIBC and NBTel, Transport Canada and Bell/ARF VideoLink
2. Consortia: OLTEC and EuroPACE 2000
3. Formal education sector applications: the Huron County Board of Education, Memorial University of Newfoundland, the University of Calgary, the Technical and Further Education Network, Laurentian University and East Carolina University
4. Minority culture and special needs applications: Special Needs Project, KAYAS Cultural College and Francophone Distance Education Networks

Case studies are typically described in terms of

1. the type of sponsoring institution
2. one particular reason the project was included in this book
3. the project's aims, participants, content, learning format, type of equipment configuration and other pertinent details
4. cost or business case information, if available
5. evaluation results if an evaluation was conducted

Then "lessons learned" are described based on telephone or e-mail interviews with someone involved in the project. Although the majority are instructors, learning designers, technical coordinators, managers and evaluators are also included. Because we believe a team approach facilitates success, we thought it important that instructors reading this book or viewing the videotape should appreciate the perspective of team colleagues. All quotations are based on these previously unpublished interviews.

The format and content differ somewhat, as the people we contacted were sometimes constrained by institutional policies in their ability to talk about their activities. Cost data are particularly variable as methods for calculating costs are different in almost every situation, and specific figures rapidly become dated and are often confidential.

Personnel from OLTEC, Laurentian University and Memorial University of Newfoundland are among those who appear on the videotape that accompanies this book.

Publications arising from the projects are provided as references if they are available even if they are not cited in the text. Because all the projects have evolved since the interviews, we provide contact names at the end of the book and recommend that you get in touch with people directly if you wish to know the project's current status.

What Themes Emerged from the Interviews?

Commonalities emerged from these interviews. We highlight five that we think apply to all learning settings.

1. Practice is essential, as familiarity with the technology is key to being able to focus on learning. Both instructors and learners need opportunities to "try it out" before turning their attention to content and learning process issues.
2. Attention to detail is critical to success. One cannot be too meticulous in double-checking and verifying as much as possible.
3. Audio quality is a greater concern than picture quality. A variety of solutions are described.
4. The way instructors should organize the timing of learning activities is different in Video Learning as compared with learning in the classroom.
5. Customized internal training materials that relate to your situation are often needed in spite of the excellent published resources that are available.

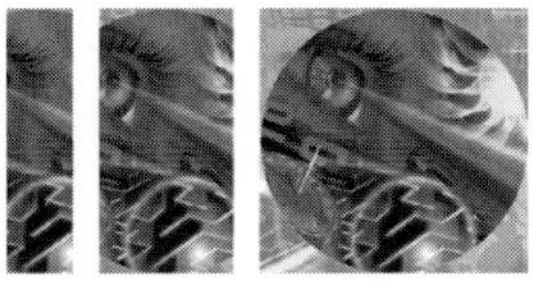

CONSULT ANOTHER BOOK IN THIS SERIES, WRITTEN BY DONALD MACDONALD OF ANTIGONISH, NOVA SCOTIA, FOR MORE DETAILS ON AUDIO SOLUTIONS THAT COULD BE ADAPTED TO VIDEO LEARNING (1998).

You will find that some issues described in the case studies relate to points made in Parts 1 and 3. While we have noted some of these relationships for you, we have given you the opportunity to identify others for yourself, and we have intentionally not cross-referenced all of them.

We suggest that you consider the following stories as illustrative of a context that might apply to you, rather than as situations unique to the institution described.

WHAT WORKPLACE EXAMPLES COULD I CONSIDER?

Remediation Training in the Financial Sector

The Canadian Imperial Bank of Commerce, Toronto, Ontario

The Canadian Imperial Bank of Commerce (CIBC) is an international bank serving over a dozen countries, with headquarters in Toronto, Ontario. This pilot project looks at the feasibility of starting with a very low-key trial within a large organization.

In the spring of 1994, CIBC's Learning Systems Group mounted a pilot project in which Video Learning was used to teach three modules on financial statements, financial accounting and taxation. These modules were part of a series of remediation training sessions being offered by the Group in response to a general test of credit knowledge and skills taken by Bank personnel in the loans and risk management departments. The project involved a partnership between Credit Risk Management (the client), the Learning Systems Group (instructional design and project management) and internal and external subject matter experts.

The Compressed Video Learning format was chosen for five reasons:

1. It was a learning option the organizers hoped would appeal to those who were chosen to participate in the session.

2. It provided a means of offering somewhat smaller "chunks" of content than had been previously offered in the classroom method.
3. It enhanced dialogue across the country.
4. It enabled the Bank to take national advantage of local expertise.
5. It was estimated that videoconferencing would reduce delivery costs compared with classroom delivery.

The purposes of the pilot were to (1) assess participant reaction to the medium, (2) experiment with the pacing and structuring requirements of the medium and (3) evaluate a particular course offering.

The content of the pilot was an existing six-hour "Quality of Financial Statements" course from an external vendor (subject matter expert). ADCOM's PictureTel equipment was operated in the six-line mode described in Chapter 3 on a point-to-point basis between two sites in Ontario. The content was offered in one 3 1/2-hour session, which was organized according to the agenda shown in Figure 4.1.

The participants were asked for their feedback at the end of the session. When compiled, the results indicated a high level of satisfaction with the format. Based on this positive feedback, two more modules were designed for Video Learning delivery. The participants completed a written evaluation form at the completion of the first module (see Figure 4.2).

Subsequent modules were adjusted to reflect this feedback. The primary design change made was to give participants more opportunity for interaction and to reduce the proportion of time spent delivering content.

The pilot project was funded from monies earmarked for remediation based on the results of the general test of credit knowledge and skills mentioned above. The pilot was estimated to cost approximately Can$3,800. Included in that total were the costs of two dry runs, lunch for the 14 participants who contributed their feedback on the experience and the fees paid to the subject matter experts.

Although this project represents a first for the Learning Systems Group, CIBC's brokerage partner, Wood Gundy, had been using videoconferencing to conduct daily meetings among several of its offices around the world to plan its stock market strategy for the day. The videoconferencing format had also been used by executives in its personal and commercial banking operations to communicate with distant staff. In other words, other sections of the bank had extensive experience with the technology before the Learning Systems Group's pilot project was mounted.

> The most important lesson that we learned from this pilot project was to be very clear with the supplier about what was required by way of technology and room setup. For example, the type of microphone and size of room provided were different from those requested. As a result, participants in the "remote" site indicated that it was difficult to hear one of the presenters well because the microphone did not pick up the sidebar conversation s/he was having with those in the room, and they felt uncomfortable as a very small group in the large auditorium that was provided.
>
> *Caroline Gray, Designer, Learning Systems, CIBC*

Financial Statement Quality

8:00 - 8:30	*Introduction:* People, technology, and protocol	
8:30 - 8:40	*Course Introduction*	- Facilitator - Participant objectives - Facilitator objectives and perspective - Course mechanics and materials
8:40 - 9:00	*Part A*	- Group discussion - Review preread case; arrive at overall assessment
9:00 - 9:05	*Part B*	- "Notice to reader/Compilation" - Facilitator
9:05 - 9:10		- Individual reading of Further Case Materials
9:10 - 9:20		- Group discussion of Further Materials
9:20 - 9:25	*Part C*	- "Review" - Facilitator
9:25 - 9:40		- Individual reading of Further Case Materials
9:40 - 10:10		- Group exercise
		BREAK
10:10 - 10:20		- Group presentations
10:20 - 10:30		- Presentation debrief - Facilitator
10:30 - 10:40	*Part D*	- "Audits" - Individual reading of course material
10:40 - 10:50		- Group discussion
10:50 - 10:55		- Summary - Facilitator
10:55 - 11:10	*Part E*	- "Reservations" - Individual reading of course material
		BREAK
11:10 - 11:20		- Facilitator debrief of reading
11:20 - 11:30	*Wrap Up*	- Facilitator reviews and summarizes material

FIGURE 4.1: Agenda for "Financial Statement Quality" course
Source: CIBC, Learning Systems Group.

1. Did the course address your training needs in the area of financial accounting as identified by the RMA?

   Yes Somewhat No

2. If you answered "No" or "Somewhat" to #1 above, what other topics would you like to see included, in order to meet your training needs?

3. How helpful did you find the prework material in enhancing your understanding of the course content?

   Very Helpful Somewhat Helpful Unhelpful

4. How helpful were the workshop and materials in achieving the objectives listed below?

CIRCLE ONE ANSWER FOR EACH STATEMENT	A Great Deal	Somewhat	Not At All
The workshop and materials helped me:			
A. Describe how the level of attestation can impact financial risk	1	2	3
B. Explain the scope and nature of the three different types of accounting engagements	1	2	3
C. Describe the types of accountants' reservations and their implications	1	2	3

5. The level of content presented was: (PLEASE CIRCLE ONE ANSWER)

   Too Difficult Too Easy Just Right

6. The length of the workshop was: (PLEASE CIRCLE ONE ANSWER)

   Too Long Too Short Just Right

7. The pacing of the workshop was: (PLEASE CIRCLE ONE ANSWER)

   Too Fast Too Slow Just Right

8. The mix of lecture and exercises was: (PLEASE CIRCLE ONE ANSWER)

   Too Much Lecture Too Many Exercises About Right

9. On a scale of 1-5, with 5 being the highest mark, how would you rate the instructor?

   1 2 3 4 5

10. How important do you think it is to have an industry professional versus an internal facilitator deliver this course?

    Very Important Somewhat Important Not Important

11. How would you rate the program overall? (PLEASE CIRCLE ONE ANSWER)

    Excellent Very Good Good Satisfactory Unsatisfactory

12. What suggestions do you have, if any, for improving the program?

____

____

____

THANK YOU FOR YOUR FEEDBACK!

FIGURE 4.2: "Financial Statement Quality" videoconference course evaluation
Source: Learning Systems Group, CIBC.

Vendor-Developed Applications for Video Learning

NBTel, Saint John, New Brunswick

NBTel (New Brunswick Telephone Co. Ltd.) serves the province of New Brunswick. NBTel has been a leader among the Stentor owner companies in adopting technology-based approaches to training, thus applying the products it sells to meet its own training needs.

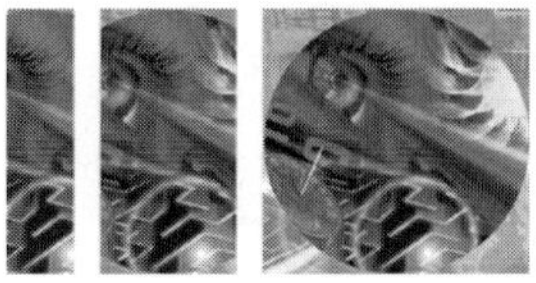

A VENDOR THAT "WALKS THE TALK" BY USING TECHNOLOGY TO MEET ITS OWN TRAINING NEEDS MAY BE MORE SENSITIVE AND RESPONSIVE TO YOUR NEEDS.

In 1993, NBTel launched its first pilot project in the application of technology-based training for its employees. Employing PictureTel technology, it offered a course in Craft Access System using dial-up videoconferencing in the two-line mode. The two-line mode continues to be used most often, although six lines are sometimes used if required to meet a session's objectives.

Currently, a variety of technology-based training approaches are used routinely to deliver course content ranging from technical skills such as Introduction to Telecommunications and Fiber Optics Appreciation to soft skills acquisition such as Facilitation and Presentation Skills. The Self-Development Centre contains a library of over 500 training materials in formats that include computers, videotapes, books and interactive videodisks.

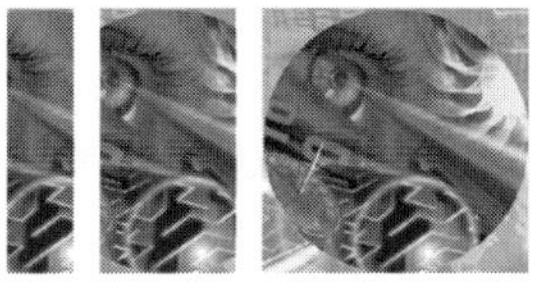

IF YOU DO NOT HAVE A SIMILAR SUPPORT FACILITY, YOU MAY WANT TO DEVELOP ONE IF YOU PLAN TO OFFER VIDEO LEARNING AS A TOOL TO SEVERAL DEPARTMENTS IN YOUR ORGANIZATION.

> Our success with videoconferencing emboldened us to try other technologies. Its ease of use is a terrific way to demystify technology-based approaches to learning and performance support.
>
> *Joyce Millican, Human Resources Support Manager, NBTel*

NBTel accords a high priority to the skills development and education of its employees. It believes that its strategic advantage comes from having well-trained and highly skilled people in the organization. NBTel allocates approximately Can$3.5 million per year to employee education and development training. Cost information for videoconferencing applications is not available.

The use of Video Learning and other technology-based strategies is coordinated through the NBTel Training Group, which provides a number of core courses in technical subjects and supports the training needs of the Sales Groups. Not only does the Training Group play a key role in delivering training courses, it also provides its internal clients with consulting services such as helping to identify skills gaps for a group or individual, sourcing and recommending education and development solutions and acting as a coordinator in setting up programs and ensuring that its clients' needs are met.

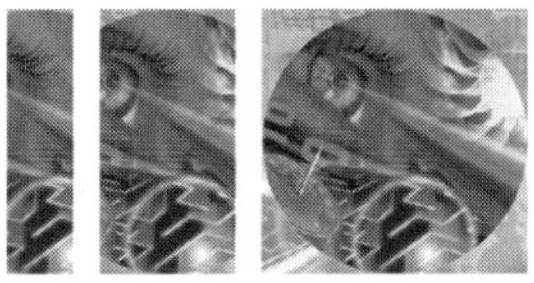

DON'T HESITATE TO FORM PARTNERSHIPS TO ACQUIRE THE EXPERTISE YOU NEED AT THE OUTSET. LIMIT THEIR SCOPE, HOWEVER, IF YOU PLAN TO OPERATE INDEPENDENTLY IN THE LONG TERM.

One of the keys to the NBTel Training Group's success has been its partnership with Forsgren & Associates, a local private training company specializing in the design of technology-based learning.

Evaluating Diverse Workplace Applications

Transport Canada, Ottawa, Ontario

In the spring of 1992, Transport Canada's Training Directorate used videoconferencing in a pilot project linking its Ottawa, Ontario, headquarters with the Canadian Coast Guard College in Sydney, Nova Scotia, a distance that requires approximately four and a half hours of travel time by air and one flight change (see Figure 4.3). This federal government case study is included here because its extensive report on that pilot project provides practical evaluation results and contains a range of materials that illustrate how diverse videoconferencing applications can be. It is also indicative of trends in many governments in other countries. The United States Government Accounting Office, for example, is an active user of Video Learning.

A recent evaluation conducted by the Transport Canada Training Directorate, Future Learning Branch, found that Video Learning was an effective and efficient tool in a learning environment for seven reasons:

1. It adds the visual aspect to two-way communication, which permits the use of visual aids and creates a "face-to-face" presence.
2. It is interactive.
3. It is easy to use, which increases the comfort level for presenters and learners.
4. It is reliable.
5. It is cost-effective.
6. It enables access to subject matter experts located elsewhere.
7. It was accepted and used by instructors, guest speakers and students alike, and more importantly, participants learned.

Although precise cost figures are not available, the Department estimates that it recovered the capital cost of the two equipment units within 12 months of their purchase through savings in travel and in time away from the workplace, especially for instructors and subject matter experts who had previously traveled to various Department locations such as the Coast Guard College. Since then, net savings have been realized. In addition, when the equipment is not used by the Training Directorate, it is used by other sections in the Department to conduct various types of meetings. These business users also report a high degree of satisfaction with this new mode of communication.

As a result of this success, a business case was made and approved for the purchase of additional videoconferencing units. As of August 1994, Transport Canada owned and operated 14 fully compatible units across Canada (see Figure 4.3). However, as a result of subsequent government reorganization and downsizing, management of the network has been contracted out to Bell Canada, which now handles all bookings and on-site user training.

The Department's system generally operates in both the two-line and six-line modes and uses a videoconferencing bridge in Ottawa that is fully dedicated to its needs. Each site is equipped with:

- two television monitors
- a microphone integrated into the keyboard for the equipment operator and small groups, with the option to add other microphones for larger groups
- a main camera pointed at the group
- a document camera
- a VCR

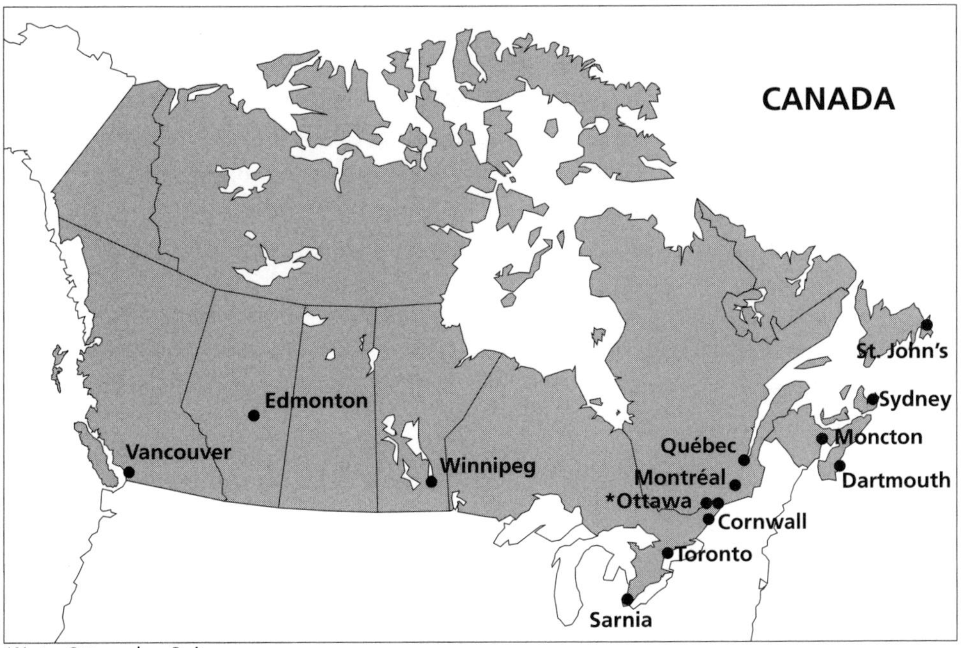

FIGURE 4.3: Transport Canada videoconferencing network

Personal computers can be integrated into the system depending on the application. If a prerecorded videotape is to be used, either multiple copies are made and one sent to each site, or the videotape is transmitted over the videoconferencing units, depending on the cost involved.

"The opportunities for using the technology are endless, and innovative applications continue to surface," reports one of the project's initiators, Louis Valois. A partial list of the Department's activities to date includes:

- conducting meetings or conferences
- conducting staffing boards
- conducting fact-finding interviews
- conducting hearings
- marketing services and products
- making announcements
- making formal introductions
- teaching and learning
- accessing expertise
- team building
- demonstrating products
- sharing scarce resources
- brainstorming

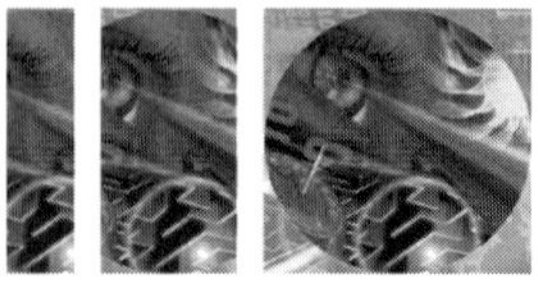

BOTH TRANSPORT CANADA AND LAURENTIAN UNIVERSITY HAVE PRODUCED CUSTOMIZED SUPPORT MATERIALS FOR THEIR USERS. OTHER ORGANIZATIONS RELY UPON EXISTING MATERIALS FROM OTHER SOURCES. APPRECIATE THE NEEDS OF YOUR USERS, AND DECIDE WHICH APPROACH TO TAKE EARLY IN YOUR PLANNING PROCESS. ANOTHER BOOK IN THIS SERIES, PREPARED BY LIZ BURGE AND JUDY ROBERTS (1998), DESCRIBES HOW TO PREPARE LEARNER GUIDES THAT SUPPORT SEVERAL LEARNING TECHNOLOGIES. IT FEATURES THE TRANSPORT CANADA MATERIAL.

A critical factor in the Network's ongoing success are the tools that have been developed to assist users. A 30-page manual has been produced to describe the use of videoconferencing for learning. "We have distributed over 400 copies and received very positive feedback," reports Louis Valois, a training specialist involved in the project from the Ottawa end. On September 25, 1995, the Coast Guard College and other Transport Canada staff (including Mr. Valois) were transferred to the Department of Fisheries and Oceans. That Department is therefore also an active user of Video Learning.

Taking Video Learning for a Test Drive: Lessons Learned

Addiction Research Foundation, Toronto, Ontario

Although the Addiction Research Foundation (ARF) Training and Education Unit began exploring Video Learning on a trial basis in early 1994, its first major use of the videoconferencing technology occurred in May 1995, when a pilot project to deliver an entire workshop by Video Learning was undertaken. The Bell/ARF VideoLink Project demonstrates the ease with which a project can be mounted using publicly available rooms equipped for videoconferencing. As we noted in an earlier chapter, the use of such rooms is one way to minimize the costs of a trial.

The four goals of the pilot project, reports Murray Richmond, then ARF's assistant director of Education and Training in Toronto, were:

1. Determine the suitability of Video Learning as a method of delivering training events.
2. Document the costs involved.
3. Identify techniques for using Video Learning effectively.
4. Suggest future opportunities for using videoconferencing at ARF.

Based on a needs assessment conducted with Thunder Bay agencies, a three-day workshop was developed entitled Overview of Basic Counselling and Assessment Techniques. Workshop content contained both knowledge and skills components and incorporated a videotape and other visual materials. Course sessions were scheduled for a full day per week over three consecutive weeks (May 3, 10 and 17, 1995) to provide a comparison with "normal" day-long classroom sessions and to offer an opportunity for homework assignments. Two very experienced trainers with no previous Video Learning experience led the workshop. Faculty were given an overview of the equipment in the videoconference room by Bell Conferencing Consultant. Participants at all sites were given an opportunity to explore the equipment at their site via introductory exercises incorporating the equipment (e.g. document camera) developed and facilitated by Ellen Lederman, ARF's distance education coordinator.

The Bell/ARF VideoLink Project connected Bell Canada sites in Thunder Bay, Sault Ste. Marie, North Bay and Toronto using the six-line mode. Twenty-five front-line addictions workers, representing a range of community agencies, participated from Bell Canada sites in the Northern Ontario communities of Thunder Bay, Sault Ste. Marie and North Bay. The instructor was located at a Bell Canada site in Toronto. A fee of Can$125, half ARF's normal rate, was charged to those who attended the workshop. While this registration fee covered incidental expenses, the bulk of the cost was absorbed by Bell Canada, which donated all the room rentals, bridging fees and long-distance costs required by the three-day event. The six-line mode was used. Figures 4.4 to 4.6 show the session agendas for each day. The videoconferencing link was maintained throughout each of the three days, so that when each group was working independently on site, communication with any other site was possible. A discussion leader was identified at each site.

The Draft Final Report written by Rob Pearson and his colleagues at ARF (1995) indicates that the direct costs absorbed by Bell totaled Can$140 per day per participant for the six-line mode, or Can$100 per day per participant if two lines were used. ARF's daily cost of offering training at that time was Can$70 per day per participant, and some portion of that $70 would have had to be added to the videoconferencing costs. However, while Video Learning seems initially more expensive than face-to-face seminars, ARF's use of Video

ADDICTION RESEARCH FOUNDATION
SCHEDULE: MAY 3, 1995
Assessment and Treatment Planning

TIME	TOPIC
9:00	• Introductions and overview • Warm-up activity
9:30	• Identification, screening and assessment differences across the continuum • Continuum of use, abuse and dependency
10:30	**BREAK**
10:45	• Assessment of substance abuse • Group case discussion
12:15	**LUNCH**
1:15	• Examples of assessment tools • How to use results effectively • Video excerpt and discussion
2:45	**BREAK**
3:00	• Treatment planning principles • Case discussion
4:00	**ADJOURN**

FIGURE 4.4: Bell/ARF Videolink Project daily agenda

ADDICTION RESEARCH FOUNDATION
SCHEDULE: MAY 10, 1995
Treatment Models and Counseling

TIME	TOPIC
9:00	• Review of session 1
9:15	• Two models of treatment
9:45	• Debrief homework assignment
10:15	**BREAK**
10:30	• Introduction to stages of change model
11:00	• Matching interventions to counseling: • precontemplation and contemplation
11:30	• Demonstration
12:00	**LUNCH**
1:00	• Practice
1:45	• Debrief
2:00	**BREAK**
2:15	• Matching interventions to counseling • preparation and action
3:00	• Developing an individual treatment plan • Assign homework and closure
4:00	**ADJOURN**

FIGURE 4.5: Bell/ARF Videolink Project daily agenda

ADDICTION RESEARCH FOUNDATION
SCHEDULE: MAY 17, 1995
Group Therapy and Family Therapy

TIME	TOPIC
9:00	• Review of session 2
9:20	• Participant feedback
9:30	• Homework assignment. Discussion at sites.
9:45	• Homework assignment. Review by site.
10:15	**BREAK**
10:30	• Introduction to group therapy
12:00	**LUNCH**
1:00	• Introduction to family therapy
2:15	**BREAK**
2:30	• Focus group
4:00	**ADJOURN**

FIGURE 4.6: Bell/ARF Videolink Project daily agenda

Learning would result in an overall cost savings to participants, who wouldn't have to travel to Toronto. Seventy percent (70%) of those responding to the course evaluation survey said they would be willing to pay higher registration fees for a course delivered by Video Learning.

Both an evaluation survey (see Appendix 1) and a focus group were held with the participants in the final session, and postsession interviews were conducted with the two trainers. Overall reactions from both groups were positive. Ninety-one percent (91%) of the respondents indicated that they would be interested in participating in future training events using videoconferencing and mentioned access to training without the need to travel as the major advantage. Having the course spread over three weeks was another factor frequently mentioned as contributing to accessibility, as participants were able to build the sessions into their schedule more easily than they could have accommodated a minimum of three consecutive days in Toronto.

As we noted in Chapter 1, most participants liked the technology, indicating that they found the Video Learning experience to be as acceptable as learning in a classroom. The technical quality of the sound, rather than picture quality, seemed to be of greatest concern to the participants, a result similar to the one reported below in the Memorial University and Huron County examples. Most participants found that their initial interactions with the faculty and other learners were awkward because the audio delay took some getting used to. However, after a few hours, the participants adapted to it.

The frequent use of other visual materials such as overheads and videotapes, along with the use of several presentation modes (lecture, question and answer, small-group activities), appeared to be appreciated more in a Video Learning session than in a traditional classroom setting. These variations seemed to facilitate the discussion of points during a presentation, something that participants did not think happened in lecture-based presentations.

The trainers felt they had to adapt their classroom style to Video Learning and found that the most difficult aspect of doing this was the absence of learners in the classroom. Unlike Sandra Hodder in the OLTEC sessions (see p. 42), these faculty members were alone in their classrooms, which seemed more like television studios, and they had difficulty feeling the presence of their students. Chapters 5 to 7 provide suggestions for overcoming these challenges.

In general, ARF's Training and Education Videoconference team recommends three strategies: incrementalism, evaluation and direct experience.

1. Careful planning and incrementalism: Starting with a small project and being able to plan and adjust over a three-week period were seen by ARF staff as being as critical to success, as was their previous experience in 1994.
2. Constant evaluation: ARF developed a list of those aspects of the technology it wished to test, created opportunities to do so, collected data continuously during the pilot and made changes as the project proceeded.
3. Direct experience with the technology: Providing faculty and participants with an opportunity to work with the technology before addressing the

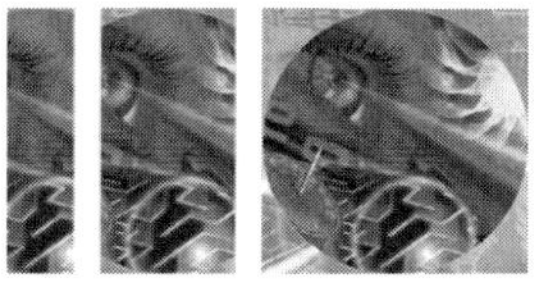

HAVING SOMEONE TO CONTROL THE CAMERA SHOTS AND SCREEN VIEWS MADE IT MUCH EASIER FOR THE TRAINERS TO CONCENTRATE ON THEIR CONTENT AND INTERACTIONS WITH THE PARTICIPANTS.

formal content would have increased the project's initial effectiveness. This is something ARF wished it had done.

One of the results of this pilot project, reports Rob Pearson, the project's instructional designer, is a predisposition to experiment with a variety of other learning technologies, and a sense throughout the organization that learning technologies have potential.

WHAT CONSORTIA MODELS COULD I APPLY TO MY SETTING?

Transferring Knowledge in Science and Engineering

Ontario Learning and Technology Exchange Consortium, Toronto, Ontario

Founded as a small working group in December 1992, the Ontario Learning and Technology Exchange Consortium (OLTEC) became a pilot project sponsored by a number of public and private sector stakeholders in southern Ontario. Its purpose was to take advantage of new opportunities offered by rapid advances in computer and communications technologies. It is included here to illustrate how Video Learning can be used at a very early stage of a consortium's development. You need not be a mature organization such as the CIBC or NBTel to experiment with Video Learning.

OLTEC's primary aim was to contribute to the improvement of the competence, knowledge and skills of engineers, scientists and technologists throughout their careers by facilitating continuous knowledge transfer through distance learning networks and technology-based approaches to learning. As a consortium, OLTEC brought together organizations from three key sectors: engineering and technology-based industries and agencies, postsecondary educational institutions, and providers of communications and information technologies. As of August 1995, OLTEC had 18 participants.

OLTEC is an illustration of changes that are occurring in many professional environments. Although engineering faculties in Canada have not traditionally used distance education extensively, many are now experimenting with technology-based approaches to graduate and undergraduate teaching, as well as to professional development. Anecdotal comments indicate that one reason for this change in behavior is that the bandwidth they feel they require is now affordable.

To achieve its objectives, OLTEC conducted a feasibility and business planning process between June and December 1994. It also mounted a Video Learning demonstration project in May-June 1995, consisting of three one-day to two-day workshops on three different topics.

For one of these workshops, compressed videoconferencing in the two-line mode was used to link three university faculty of engineering sites to one corporate site in the Sheridan Science and Technology Park, Mississauga, Ontario. The universities (McMaster, Waterloo and Toronto) developed their own videoconferencing network, "Engineering Remote Classroom Network (ERCnet)," at the same time as OLTEC was developing. Companies such as Xerox and Atomic Energy of Canada Ltd. (AECL) in Sheridan Park already had videoconferencing facilities because their corporations each had in-house networks. The ERCnet facilities, loaned and supported by the three universities, used PictureTel equipment purchased from ADCOM Inc. The Sheridan Park site, hosted by Xerox Corporation, was also equipped with PictureTel equipment purchased as part of a multipoint corporate network managed by Xerox in the United States. OLTEC thus kept its costs low by using existing installations in its university and corporate partner sites, which were made available to OLTEC at no charge.

Approximately 20 people from OLTEC's member universities and companies registered for the first workshop. They were distributed over the four sites shown in Figure 4.7.

Sandra Hodder, program coordinator at the School of Computing and Information Management at Sheridan College in Oakville, Ontario, gave the course, which was entitled Project Management Tools and Techniques. She has taught this subject many times as a one-day, face-to-face workshop in which the effective teaching time was approximately six hours. She and a team from ERCnet adapted it to two three-hour videoconferencing sessions. Sandra shared "tips from a novice videoconference instructor," some of which are highlighted in the videotape accompanying this book.

Preparation was critical. Sandra developed an 80-page course manual based on the one she normally used in the classroom. It was designed to provide one page for every point made in the course, with lots of white space so that

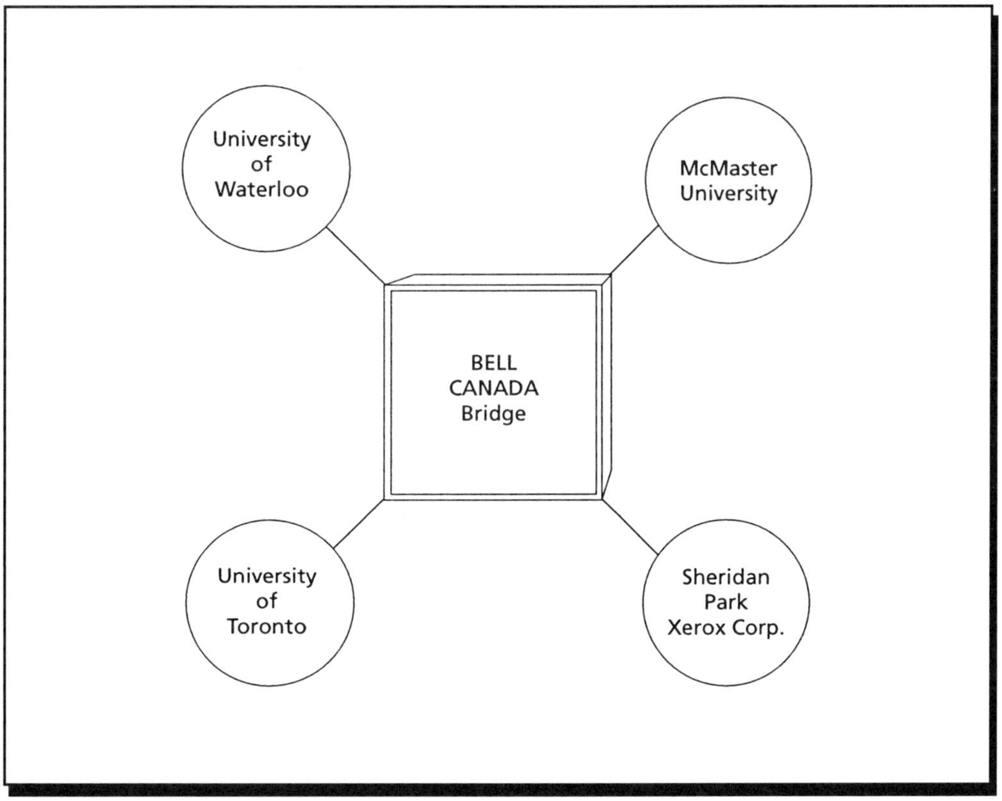

FIGURE 4.7: Sites linked in OLTEC first Pilot Trial course

students could make notes on each page. Three differences in preparing the material for the videoconference, rather than for the classroom, were: (1) more pages were prepared for the videoconference, so that everything would be clear for the learners, (2) pages to be transmitted by the document camera had to be redesigned and (3) pages that could not be easily transmitted by the document camera *had* to be in the manual—if something like a detailed computer printout was in the manual, Sandra could easily refer to it by page number.

A sample of the visuals was tested in a point-to-point "rehearsal" session organized by the University of Toronto Media Centre. Factors tested included background color, size of illustrations, and type and size of font.

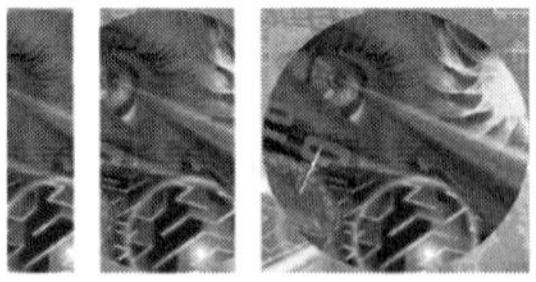

REMEMBER THE CIBC'S REFERENCE TO TWO DRY RUNS? REFER BACK TO THIS SECTION WHEN READING THE SECTION IN CHAPTER 6 ON THE IMPORTANCE OF PREPARATION.

> Spontaneity is clearly possible with videoconferencing, but, from my experience, I would suggest that a high degree of spontaneity is only possible over time, when both the instructor and the students are familiar with the technology and with one another. That said, don't be afraid to "be yourself."

In adapting visuals for the camera, we had to reformat them for the camera's three-by-four aspect ratio, as well as simplify the content so that it would be easily understood at the other end. "I found that presenting a 'simple' graphic worked well, as it motivated students to listen to what I had to add. I felt it contributed to holding their attention." Examples of the differences between the print version of a visual in the student manual and the same visual shown under the document camera or an overhead transparency are given in Appendix 2, as they are too big to replicate here.

> The videoconference technology lends itself to the lecture mode, which I felt had to be avoided if I were to facilitate learning. I have an interactive teaching style in the classroom, which I comfortably replicated in the OLTEC Trial once I adapted to the technology.

The little things make a difference. Sandra found that the control console at the host site was too high, making it difficult for her to reach the button that switched from the camera pointed at her to the document camera. On the first day, she used a pencil to make the switch; on the second day, the technical staff brought her a pointer, which was longer and made switching easier.

In the first of the two three-hour sessions, two of Sandra's colleagues timed the session and noted that the pace of the videoconference was slower than that of a classroom. "We estimated that, because of the time spent in activities such as alternating between the two cameras and waiting for responses to questions, we lost approximately 25 percent of our learning time." As a result, one of the course's four main modules was assigned as a self-study unit and was not reviewed in class. Three three-hour sessions (nine hours) would have been needed to discuss all four modules as a group. "The interactivity simply takes more time. However, as participants become more used to the technology, waits may be fewer."

> I don't do much warm-up or ice-breaking at the start of a one-day seminar. I find that participants want me to start the content right away as they want to get a feel for the content and the environment. I usually wait until after the first coffee break before I try an activity such as polling people for their

names. I would not alter that approach in the Video Learning mode, but I would have appreciated receiving a list of the names and corporate affiliations of participants in advance. It would have assisted me in developing a feel for the group.

Participating in OLTEC helped members identify their Video Learning needs. Many members are continuing to use this approach to better serve learners, reports Michael Charles, dean of the University of Toronto's Faculty of Applied Science and Engineering.

Minimizing Costs in a Transnational Consortium for Graduate Education

EuroPACE 2000, Heverlee, Belgium

Founded in 1993, EuroPACE 2000 is a trans-European consortium of universities and their partners in education and training whose goal is to demonstrate the potential of information and communications technologies for the European universities of the future. EuroPACE 2000's membership currently consists of over 45 universities, more than seven enterprises and research institutions, and eight regional, national or international organizations.

EuroPACE 2000 works on a partnership model with its members; it provides several technical platforms and instructional models while its members develop all the programs. The programs are concentrated in five areas: (1) Ph.D. programs, where the goals are to train researchers by pooling scarce resources in Centres of Excellence and creating joint degrees, and to facilitate knowledge transfer from Centres of Excellence to industry; (2) advanced professional degree programs and continuing education designed to update professionals in their own discipline or to train them in new skills that their employers define as needed; (3) open discussion groups and professional and academic television designed for public broadcasting distribution for the general television viewership; (4) customized programs made on demand; and (5) a tutoring service offered by computer conferencing to support the other four programs.

"We want to improve the science and technology literacy of those in educational institutions, the workplace and the general public," notes Jef Van den Branden, educational director at EuroPACE 2000's office in Heverlee, Belgium.

Compressed videoconferencing, alone or in combination with technologies ranging from print to satellite television, is a significant feature of the technical infrastructure supporting these programs. Thirty sites (of a total of about 250 which EuroPACE 2000 manages) are equipped with this technology; the aim is that by the end of 1997 at least 100 sites will be using this technology. While any organization with appropriate equipment is welcome to join a given program, the EuroPACE 2000 centers are established to serve those who do not have their own equipment. "Although costs are coming down, we and our members still feel that there is a role for a consortium such as ours because it minimizes the costs," reports Jef Van den Branden. While an annual membership of 2000 Ecu is not cheap, it is enormously cost-effective when the alternative is considered. Membership entitles a member to free use of all EuroPACE 2000 facilities, although collaborating educational institutions will still charge their normal tuition fees.

Jef reports that videoconferencing is particularly suited to the Ph.D. programs and live programs, such as the open discussion groups, for three reasons:

1. Seeing the other participants in the group makes the learners feel more comfortable accessing each other. EuroPACE's experience is that videoconferencing technology stimulates learners to communicate more freely with one another.
2. The equipment has become affordable for institutions and even for individuals, the technology is stable as long as standards are respected, and videoconferencing is as easy to use as making a telephone call.
3. Obtaining digital telephone lines from providers is no longer problematic in most European countries. As videoconferencing in its lower level (two-line mode) costs only twice as much as a normal long-distance call, communication costs are very reasonable.

One particularly good example of the use of videoconferencing is a recent transnational course entitled Advanced Computer Science designed for an audience of graduate and postgraduate students at university research centers and for researchers in corporate environments. After an interactive satellite broadcast linked 14 sites, a series of six multipoint Compressed Video Learning seminars was held that connected the six universities directly involved in the Ph.D. course. Each of these Video Learning seminars followed a similar format. After a top expert reviewed the subject in lecture mode, using graphics and illustrative demonstrations where appropriate (about 45 minutes), an interactive discussion occurred between the lecturer and participants for another 45 minutes. A computer conferencing service facilitated discussion between the seminars and delivered handouts to the participants. A total of 32 Ph.D. students attended the full series of "broadcast plus seminars"; approximately 30 other people participated in the broadcast but not the seminars.

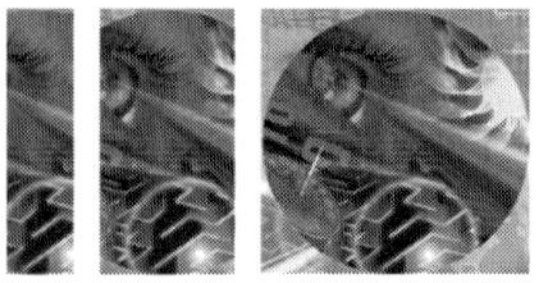

"COMMUNICATION WILL NOT TAKE PLACE AUTOMATICALLY; IT MUST BE CAREFULLY PREPARED AND ANIMATED. THE TECHNOLOGY FACILITATES THE INTERACTION, BUT CAN ALSO INHIBIT IT OR EVEN TURN IT INTO CHAOS WHEN BADLY USED." (JEF VAN DEN BRANDEN, EDUCATIONAL DIRECTOR, EUROPACE 2000)

The advantages that such a course offers are multiple. Students gain access to expertise that goes beyond what is available at their campuses, as do workplace professionals. Having direct access for a considerable time to experts who otherwise can only be known through their publications or by seeing them at a single conference is a major benefit. The transnational exchange of information and ideas adds an extra dimension and creates a potential for future transborder cooperation. Companies can offer their employees a quick update in one or more topics in their field. An environment in which one can hear and see the other participants stimulates communication.

These advantages, however, may turn into disadvantages if a basic consideration is overlooked: the equipment is only a tool.

One specific challenge to orderly interaction can occur when switching between various sites in multipoint videoconferencing. The switching is typically sound-driven—the bridge connecting the sites selects the site that has requested the floor. However, the bridge cannot distinguish between "approved noise" generated by a participant's comment and "unintended noise" generated by shuffling papers or side conversations. Jef reports that "it is therefore a good idea to have at each site a tutor or animator who is previously briefed about these issues and the seminar's agenda. This tutor can assist the seminar moderator by, for example, monitoring the local site for unintended noise, by facilitating discussion when questions are called for and by managing on-site activity when a technical problem occurs—which of course will happen now and then!"

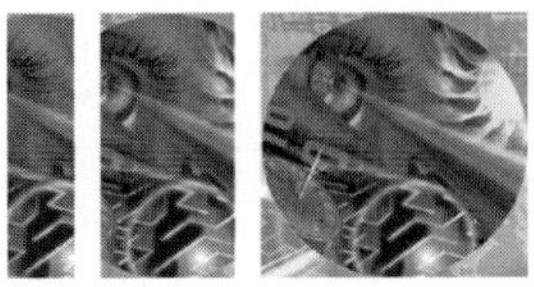

OTHER CHALLENGES AND SOLUTIONS TO COMMUNICATION AND LEARNING ARE DESCRIBED IN PART 3.

HOW ARE SCHOOLS, COLLEGES AND UNIVERSITIES USING VIDEO LEARNING?

Changing the Mindset: A Pilot Project

The Huron County Board of Education, Clinton, Ontario

In the summer of 1994, the Huron County Board of Education in southwestern Ontario agreed to participate in a pilot project to explore ways in which Video Learning could be used in elementary and secondary schools. Its experience in 1994-95 illustrates one way organizations can assess the cost effectiveness of Video Learning—collaboration with a vendor.

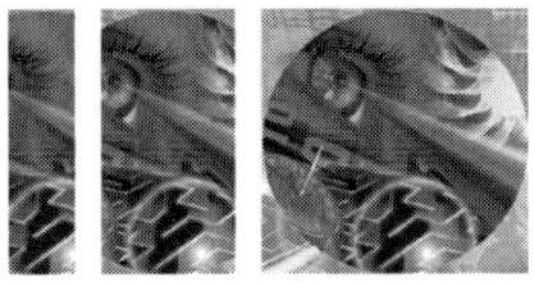

IT MAY BE WORTH EXPLORING WHETHER VENDORS IN YOUR AREA ARE OPEN TO SIMILAR PARTNERSHIPS. BEFORE APPROACHING THEM, YOU MAY NEED TO RESEARCH HOW THEIR EQUIPMENT IS CURRENTLY USED, AND DEVELOP A BUSINESS CASE JUSTIFYING WHY THEY SHOULD INVEST RESOURCES AT YOUR INSTITUTION.

The Board's applications also indicate the technology's increasing availability internationally and the way in which it can facilitate global learning events.

Located on the shores of Lake Huron, the Huron County Board of Education administers 30 schools that are spread over 4,000 square kilometers. The two schools selected to participate in the project were Central Huron Secondary School in Clinton and Goderich District Secondary School in Goderich. Clinton and Goderich are two towns of 3,000 to 5,000 people each, located approximately 20 kilometers apart.

The project was initiated by ADCOM Inc., a Toronto-based Canadian distributor of PictureTel equipment. Subsequent to a formal agreement signed on August 31, 1994, the equipment was installed on November 8, 1994.

ADCOM provided two System 4000 PictureTel units to the Board, which the Board has since purchased. The only change: "We will get a different sound system than the built-in microphone that came with the unit," says Stephen.

Stephen Oliver, a classroom teacher and technology consultant, was seconded half time by the Board to facilitate applications. From November 1994 to June 1995, the Board's Video Learning activities included:

1. several one-hour meetings with Ministry of Education officials in Toronto on "routine" school business
2. a Drama Club session with the Massachusetts Institute of Technology-based author of a play the club planned to produce

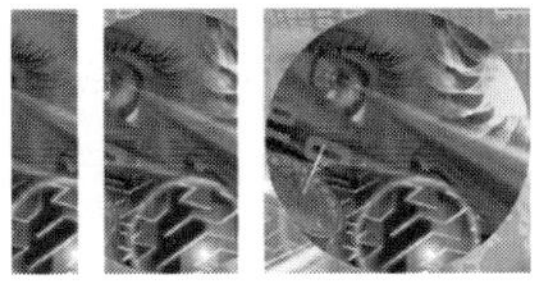

"BE SURE TO DOUBLE-CHECK ON THE AVAILABILITY OF DIGITAL SERVICE IN THE SITES THAT YOU WANT TO SERVE AND ON THE IDENTITY OF THE SERVICE PROVIDER. WE HAD TO WORK WITH BOTH BELL CANADA AND AN INDEPENDENT LOCAL TELEPHONE COMPANY TO OBTAIN THE SERVICE THAT WAS NOT READILY AVAILABLE AT THAT TIME. OUR PROJECT TIMETABLE HAD TO BE ADJUSTED ACCORDINGLY." (STEPHEN OLIVER, TECHNOLOGY CONSULTANT, HURON COUNTY BOARD OF EDUCATION)

3. a one-time friendship link with elementary students at a school in the United Kingdom
4. professional development sessions with teachers in the Perth/Huron-Perth Separate Board of Education using equipment supplied by another vendor, CBCI Telecom Inc., which is now part of Tandberg Canada Inc.
5. teaching a high school English course in the winter semester between the two schools in Goderich and Clinton

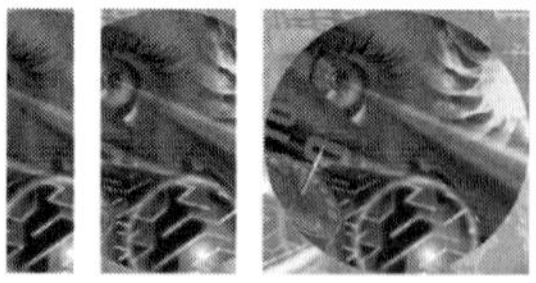

In Stephen's view, backup telephone numbers are particularly important when three or more sites are involved and a videoconferencing bridge is used.

Although no formal assessment was made, a number of lessons were learned, which Stephen shared in a telephone interview. Being a teacher of a Digital Media Studies course, Stephen was particularly aware of the technical lessons learned in the trial:

1. Ensure that the power and telephone outlets are close together so wires do not snake in different directions.
2. In a tiered classroom such as in Figure 4.8, light from windows can reflect off the television monitors if they are not positioned appropriately.
3. A readily accessible backup telephone line for voice communication is needed in the event of problems with the digital lines.

Stephen described the layout shown in Figure 4.8 as follows:

> A three-tiered rectangular room with windows along two walls. All furniture is easily moved to accommodate small discussion groups and informal videoconferencing. No problem viewing image on TVs. All windows have blinds to black out room when needed and school PA system can be disabled when an outside conference is in progress. Before acquiring Virtuoso microphones, sound was sometimes a problem and we often mounted microphones on the ceiling.

Stopping the normal school bells and announcements from being heard in the room used for the Video Learning sessions was also important so that those sounds were not transmitted to the other sites. These may be issues you would like to cross-reference with our discussion of room requirements in Chapter 3.

We raised three other non-technical issues with Stephen:

1. What about the students? What did they think of their schools' decision to experiment with the new technology? "They had no problem using the equipment, which they routinely looked after (turned on and off, adjusted, moved about) without a teacher being present."
2. And the slightly jerky motion that results with the two-line mode? "NEVER a problem for either the teachers or the students."
3. What about technical training for those involved? "Teacher and learner training to use the equipment consisted of a short one-time setup instruction session and ongoing informal advice."

Since the pilot project, a senior level calculus course and professional development sessions for teachers have occurred. The Board is also experimenting with desktop Video Learning and other modalities such as the World Wide

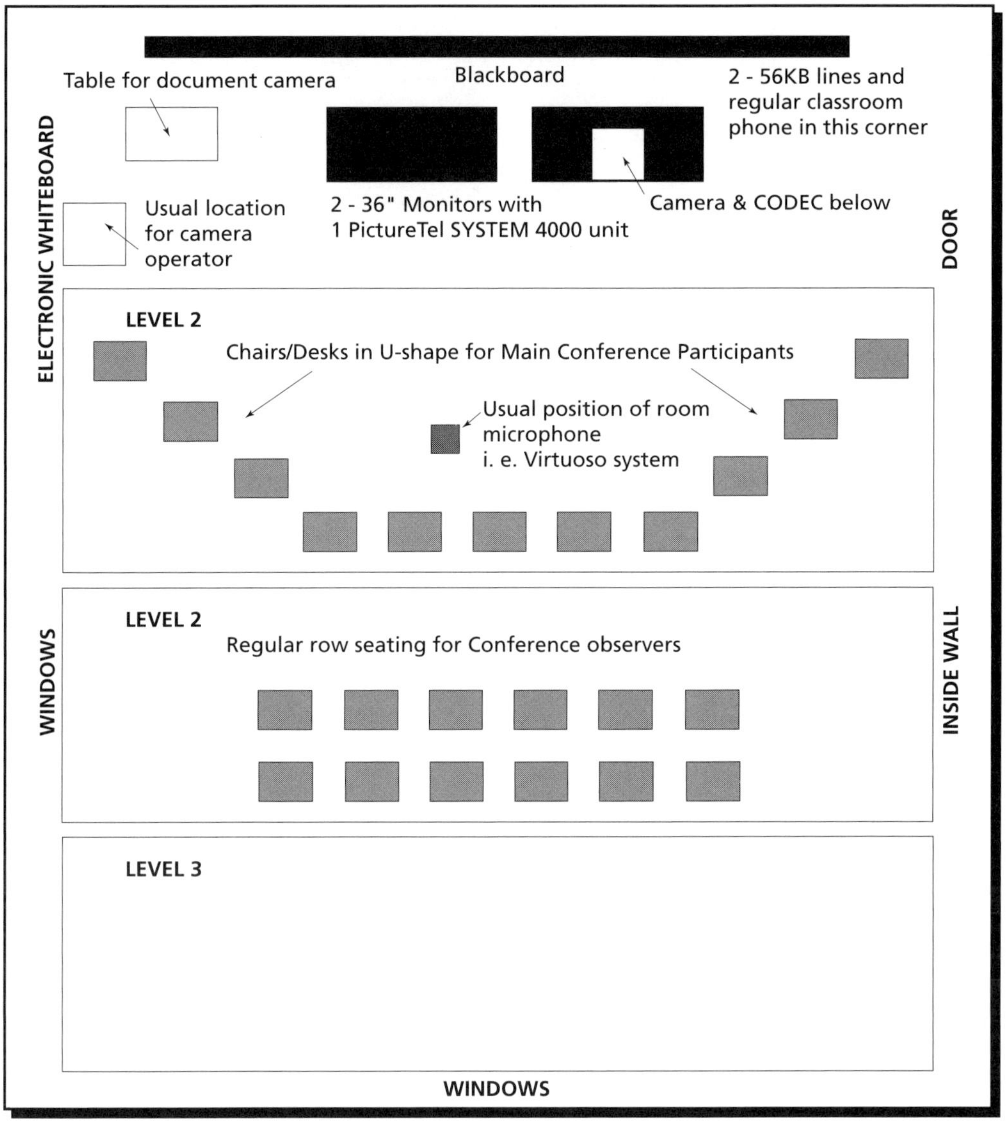

FIGURE 4.8: Huron County videoconference room layout

Web. Stephen shares one last thought regarding the fundamental challenge facing the Board and other learning professionals: "The distance in distance education is not the challenge; it's devising curriculum that is really educational."

Meeting the Needs of Stakeholders in Health and Education

Memorial University of Newfoundland, St. John's, Newfoundland and Labrador

The Telemedicine Centre and the Telemedicine and Educational Technology Resources Agency (TETRA) at Memorial University of Newfoundland in St. John's have been experimenting with Video Learning since 1992. They want to determine if and how the technology can enhance their existing interactive audiographic network, which links over 200 sites in more than 140 communities throughout the province of Newfoundland and Labrador. The University's activities demonstrate collaboration between health and educational agencies, thus showing that the same equipment can serve the needs of a diverse set of stakeholders.

Such sharing makes the purchase and operation of videoconferencing equipment cost-effective. While prices have obviously changed since Telemedicine/TETRA acquired its two videoconferencing units, the principle underlying the business case has not: it is important to conduct applications research to enhance client services.

Applications the University has tried to date include:

1. social work and pharmacy courses between St. John's and Corner Brook, the two largest cities in the province, which are located approximately one hour's flying time or six hour's driving time apart
2. pharmacy intern meetings with faculty advisors between St. John's and Corner Brook
3. continuing medical education seminars between St. John's and Corner Brook and St. John's and Calgary
4. interviews for business administration and engineering student work-term placements in cooperative education programs involving several cities in Canada (St. John's, Vancouver, Calgary) and Harlow, England
5. clinical consultations in occupational therapy, nursing, neurology and physiotherapy
6. meetings of health care professionals and other groups

All applications used Compression Lab International (CLI) equipment, generally in the six-line mode.

The staff at Telemedicine/TETRA who coordinated this diverse range of activities made a number of points when asked to reflect on "lessons learned" that would be useful for those who are just starting Video Learning applications. Their team response highlights six issues.

1. Generous start-up time: The dilemma is how much buffer time is needed for testing, especially when university and college calendar dates create pressure: "We're not sure of the answer, but the question is vitally important."
2. Camera technique: New users may want to pan (move the camera) to show shots from all over the room, without realizing the effect this has on the comfort of the viewers at other sites. Let them learn by doing: "When we showed them the effect of the camera acrobatics from our site, they soon adopted a more judicious use of that feature of the technology."
3. Facilities: Camera angle and mobility, lighting, camera lens and furniture were all issues when the same room was used for multiple applications. Camera lenses and lighting that were appropriate for one application were not necessarily suitable for the next session.
4. Instructor and learner training: "One of our biggest challenges was to convince people that there are right and wrong ways to use the technology and that training is the way to bridge the gap."

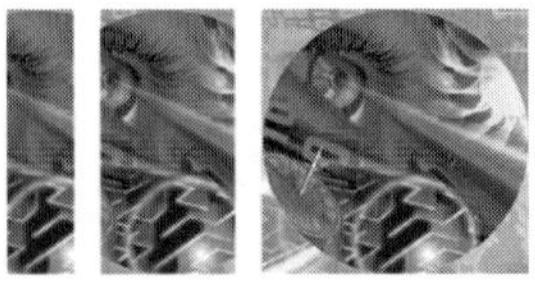

WHEN CHOOSING A VIDEOCONFERENCING SYSTEM, TRY TURNING THE VIDEO MONITORS OFF SO YOU CAN JUDGE THE AUDIO ON ITS OWN MERITS. IF YOU ARE NOT HAPPY, YOUR USERS WON'T BE EITHER!

5. Learner attitudes: Students at the remote sites tended to be more accepting of the technology's limitations than were the students on-site with the instructor. A factor in this may have been the need to use a microphone when the instructor was right in front of them!
6. The biggest problem: The audio. Poor audio led to decreased attention and frustration. The problem was not the state of the art, but the cost of the art.

Other faculties at Memorial University have since acquired at least three more videoconferencing units, and Video Learning is now regarded as a "somewhat routine" approach at the institution. Those of you with a technical interest might want to know that the next Video Learning frontier the University is crossing is videoconferencing on the Internet.

Offering a Graduate Course in Engineering

The University of Calgary, Calgary, Alberta

In the fall of 1992, the Centre for Distance Learning and Innovative Technologies of the University of Calgary, in cooperation with the Transportation Groups of the Departments of Civil Engineering at the University of Calgary and the University of Alberta, mounted a pilot project that delivered a graduate engineering course using videoconferencing. The project is reported here because the accompanying evaluation was particularly detailed (see Chapter 8) and because there was a broad experience with two-, four- and six-line types of transmission.

The technology initially used in the two-line mode linked students and instructors in Edmonton and Calgary. The course was delivered in 14 three-hour sessions and was taught on a team basis by four professors at the University of Alberta and three at the University of Calgary. The classes were held once a week and were attended by 12 students in Calgary and 16 in Edmonton. Costs were minimal. AGT, the province's largest telephone company, donated its videoconferencing facilities and did not charge for room or equipment rental, or for the long-distance costs. University instructors waived the honorarium that they would have received for teaching a distance education course.

The purpose of the evaluation was to determine the viability of videoconferencing as a distance education technology and to find out how effective the learning and teaching process was. The evaluation explored how comfortable the instructors and students were with the technology, teaching techniques that worked and those that didn't, ease of use and preparation time. The evaluation was carried out by means of student and instructor questionnaires, as well as interviews with instructors.

The results indicated that, regardless of the weaknesses perceived by both the students and instructors, the majority of them would not hesitate to learn and teach through videoconferencing again.

The evaluation results are discussed in more detail in Chapter 8. Here, we pass along five practical tips for the successful use of videoconferencing that emerged from the data.

1. Instructor workshop: The instructors must have in-service training to understand the capacity of the technology, its interactivity and the need to modify traditional classroom teaching styles.
2. Student orientation: The students need to be briefed, especially on the interactivity of the technology. They should also be permitted to meet one another through videoconferencing before the formal instruction begins.
3. Session length: Three hours is too long; two hours would be better.
4. Physical environment: The seating arrangement should be conducive to communication and interaction. It should be flexible enough to be reconfigured depending on the number of students in the class.
5. Sound quality: Adequate audio equipment is essential, and all microphones must be strategically positioned.

In September 1994, the Centre for Distance Learning set up two permanent Video Learning classrooms and now offers courses in a variety of disciplines in collaboration with several institutions in Alberta. Capital costs were funded through normal university budgeting processes. In the fall semester of 1995, approximately 10 courses at the undergraduate and master's levels were taught using compressed videoconferencing.

> We have experimented with different numbers of digital telephone lines and now believe that four lines is the most cost-effective solution for our needs. We felt that the two lines we used in 1992 did not give us the resolution we needed, and so we opted to pay the extra long-distance costs involved in using six lines. When a technical problem unexpectedly forced us to go from six to four lines, we did not notice any significant difference in the quality! We now use four lines and save one-third of our long-distance costs!
>
> *Irena Kirek, Manager,*
> *Centre for Distance Learning*
> *and Innovative Technologies*

This savings in long-distance costs is critical, since videoconferencing is the most expensive of any of the learning technology options available to the Centre. Video Learning is therefore not used for every course, but only for those courses in which the visual element is required because of the nature of the content being taught. The University considers the cost to be justified because of the value offered to the students.

One other interesting point is that the University is also using another type of videoconferencing technology, a high-speed experimental type called Asynchronous Transfer Mode (ATM). One of the two Video Learning classrooms mentioned above is equipped with this technology; experience with the technology is described in a paper written by University researcher Daesler-Lohmueller (1995).

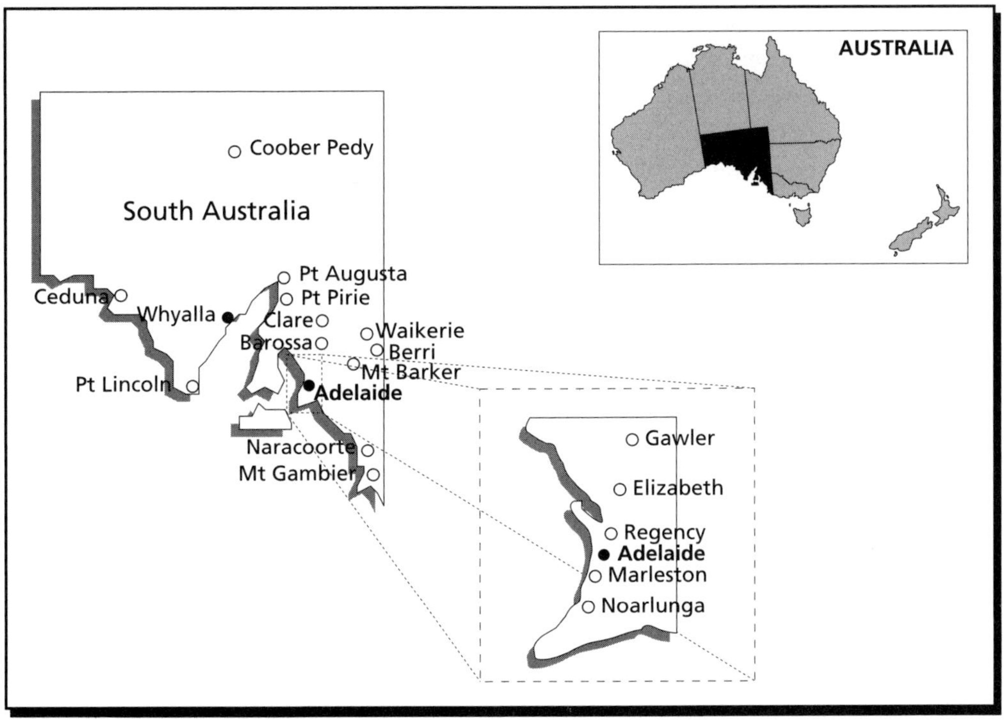

FIGURE 4.9: Map of TAFE videoconference sites

Learning from a Mature College Network

South Australian Department of Employment, Technical and Further Education, Adelaide, Australia

South Australia's Technical and Further Education (TAFE) network now links sites throughout the state. South Australia is a small state in terms of population (1.2 million), but its area is large, almost twice the area of France, or one-tenth the area of the United States. We include the network in the book because it is one of the more mature videoconferencing networks in the world and focuses exclusively on college-level programs.

After trials that began in February 1990 following two years of preparation, TAFE started in 1993 with three sites. Its goal is to share the resources of larger metropolitan institutes (those with a student body of 20,000, including part-time and distance education students) with institutes in more rural areas. The rural institutes cover considerable territory and have multiple campuses, as well as informal study centers that are extensions of the main campus. Eight of South Australia's 10 institutes now participate in the network. Programs at the certificate, associate diploma and diploma level (up to two or three years) are delivered over the network in subjects such as business studies, languages, tourism, customer service and sales techniques, rural property planning, advanced building techniques, French for winemakers and wine appreciation. "We generally operate in the two-line mode and find the resolution adequate for both the point-to-point and multipoint courses which we offer," reports Network Manager, Paul Rixon, who is based in Adelaide. "We chose

"THE MOST IMPORTANT LESSON WE HAVE LEARNED IS TO FOCUS ON OUR CORE BUSINESS – PROVIDING COURSES TO STUDENTS IN A WAY WHICH MAKES THEM FEEL COMFORTABLE AND WHICH THEY RECOGNIZE AS BEING VIABLE AND EFFICIENT." (PAUL RIXON, MANAGER, TAFE)

compressed videoconferencing because students and staff found it easy to adapt to and non-threatening to use."

One of the reasons for establishing the network was a concern about the inability to offer a wide-enough range of courses in appropriate areas of the state in ways the students felt comfortable with. Within two years of introducing videoconferencing into certain programs between then Adelaide College and the four regional sites served by Light College, student completion rates increased fivefold according to a 1993 study cited by Colin Latchem (1995), a researcher at Curtin University in Perth, Australia. "We believe these results are indicative of the rates in many of the other college programs we distribute," says Paul Rixon.

TAFE's Tele-Learning Consortium is managed by a staff of four. Its mandate is to run the network and provide training for both the teaching and support staff in the institutes that offer the courses. Each institute arranges with a central booking service to distribute its courses over the network.

TAFE's Tele-Learning Consortium placed second in 1995 in an annual international Best Practices Competition sponsored by PictureTel Corporation in the United States.

Customizing Faculty Training Programs

Laurentian University, Sudbury, Ontario

Laurentian University is a bilingual institution located in Sudbury, Ontario, and is one of two universities in Northern Ontario, a region that has 90 percent of the province's land mass and only 10 percent of its population. We summarize its faculty training activities to highlight the issue of customizing institutional services, even though equivalent types of support may be available from partners.

Laurentian collaborates with many postsecondary institutions (the University of Ottawa, Glendon College, Collège Boréal, Le Collège des Grands Lacs and Cité Collégiale) and distance education networks (Contact North/Contact Nord and the Franco-Ontarian Distance Education Network) that view Video Learning as central to their plans and that provide a wide range of instructor training and support services to their members. Undergraduate or graduate degree programs in which Laurentian makes use of Video Learning include speech pathology, business administration, midwifery, nurse practitioner, education, cinema and mathematics.

"WE FEEL THAT WE CANNOT OFFER OUR FACULTY, STAFF AND LEARNERS TOO MANY OPPORTUNITIES TO LEARN ABOUT THE EFFECTIVE USE OF VIDEOCONFERENCING. TO SUPPLEMENT THE GENERIC TRAINING OFFERED BY OUR PARTNERS, WE HAVE ADDITIONAL CUSTOMIZED TRAINING SO THAT WE ARE PART OF THE SOLUTION TO SUCCESSFUL TEACHING AND LEARNING THROUGH VIDEOCONFERENCING." (DENIS MAYER, DIRECTOR OF STUDENT AFFAIRS, LAURENTIAN UNIVERSITY)

Laurentian takes a proactive approach to faculty support and supplements the work of its partners with its own internal resources. The Centre for Continuing Education has prepared its own guide for Laurentian faculty members so that they may take advantage of the opportunities Video Learning offers. The Centre also gives workshops based on the guide so that faculty members and staff can actually use the equipment and discuss the guide with colleagues and resource personnel from the Centre before their course starts. For example, faculty members appreciate the chance to try the control tablet shown in Figure 2.4.

Denis allocates funds from the Continuing Education budget to pay for a one-day or two-day seminar each semester for anyone planning to use Video Learning for the first time in the coming term and for the distribution of Continuing Education's Video Learning guide. On-demand assistance is available at any time during the year.

Supporting an Institution's Mission through Video Learning

East Carolina University, Greenville, North Carolina

East Carolina University serves a part of North Carolina that could be characterized as rural and underserved. The University's commitment to partnerships and to Video Learning as a central tool that supports its mission is the primary reason for its inclusion in this book.

> Our Big Lesson? There needs to be partnership and institutional commitment from the top down. Faculty and staff, content and technical specialists all need to function as a team for Video Learning to be successful!
>
> *Diana Henshaw,*
> *Director, Continuing Studies, East Carolina University*

The two types of Video Learning applications at the University are the classroom model and the desktop model.

NILEC (the Network for Interactive Learning of Eastern Carolina) is the multi-mode backbone network for classroom applications. REACH-TV Network (Rural Eastern Carolina Health Television) is the medical arm of NILEC and is used for both classroom and consultation applications.

NILEC's main focus is the delivery of summer school and extension programs in the evening to its 45-site network in the state. Extension courses include topics as diverse as nursing, social work and industry and technology. NILEC has also organized international sessions in collaboration with the Sprint Meeting Channel. For example, engineering education sessions have taken place between East Carolina University in Greenville, North Carolina, and the University of Helsinki in Finland. Corporate partners include Black & Decker, which has used the network to train industrial engineers.

Telemedicine applications occur during the day on REACH-TV, when patients and staff are in hospitals and clinics. The applications focus on consultations involving over 16 different medical specialties located at the University and its four teaching hospitals. Eight outlying clinics and hospitals are linked to the network, which can be booked for consultations any time between 7 a.m. and 7 p.m., five days a week. Two sites provide emergency care 24 hours a day, seven days a week. An average of 10 consultations occur every week. Continuing education programs are also offered for physicians, nurses and other health professionals.

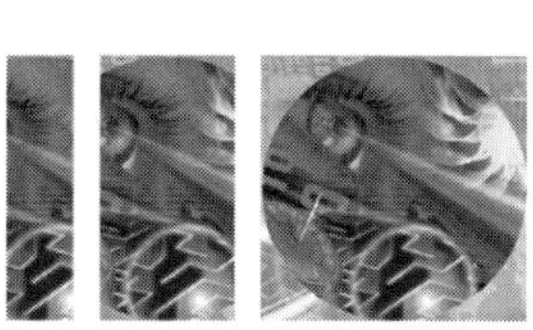

TIME SHARING IS THE FEATURE THAT HAS ENABLED THE PROFESSIONALS IN HEALTH AND EXTENSION SERVICES TO AFFORD VIDEOCONFERENCING TECHNOLOGY.

Savings are being realized in the form of time and travel costs. For example, a 1994 financial audit of a prison project found cost savings significant enough to justify considering expanding the pilot to other prison systems in the state.

Another partnership exists between the University and its two suppliers of videoconferencing technology, PictureTel and Compression Labs International (CLI). "We have had no problem interconnecting the two systems and have benefited from an impressive level of collaboration between the two vendors in meeting our needs," reports Ron Rouse, chief communications engineer of REACH-TV. "We have seven CLI and three PictureTel units in the REACH-TV network. Medical consultations use the point-to-point mode, while the continuing education sessions generally average five sites per session in the multipoint mode. The minimum speed used in any of these applications is the six-line mode, with higher speeds used when high picture quality is required."

Diana Henshaw, director of the Division of Continuing Studies, views the training of faculty and staff in all the University's colleges and faculties as central to implementing Video Learning successfully across the entire institution.

"We emphasize and share the 'in the trenches' experience which we have all acquired," notes Diana, who has herself taught courses using Video Learning techniques. "We emphasize how important it is to 'relax and enjoy'; we don't have to try to be a professional television star!" Diana offers us seven elements that she believes are critical to quality Video Learning:

1. the active engagement of learners
2. a variety of instructional approaches
3. instructors who know the content and are entertaining and personable
4. instructors who will adapt to Video Learning
5. effective support structures for both instructors and students
6. a team approach to course design
7. systematic evaluation

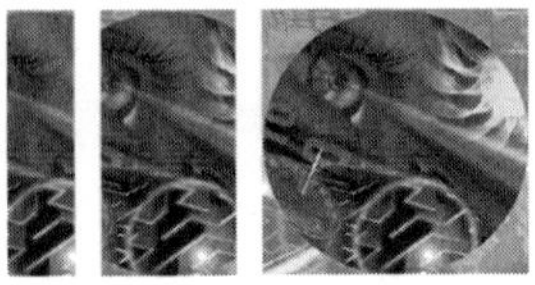

PROFESSORS WHO HAVE BEEN THROUGH THE TRAINING PROGRAMS BECOME MENTORS TO OTHERS IN THEIR FACULTY OR COLLEGE. THE DIVISION AGGRESSIVELY USES TECHNOLOGIES SUCH AS PRINT, VIDEOTAPES, AND THE INTERNET OR COMPUTER BULLETIN BOARD SERVICES TO DEVELOP AND PROVIDE CONTINUING SUPPORT TO A CORPS OF TRAINED MENTORS.

As it works to ensure that these elements are in place throughout the institution, East Carolina University looks optimistically toward the future. Diana Henshaw (1995) and her colleague, David Balch, summarized their views in a paper they presented at the International Council for Distance Education conference in Birmingham: "We are riding down the information highway into the twenty-first century. There may well be curves, hills, and detours along the way. We have no clear map to guide us. But ... we have a vision of the new world and we are embarking on the journey with a sense of enthusiasm and adventure" (p. 111).

The University also has a desktop Video Learning application. The Department of Industrial Technology in the School of Industry and Technology has mounted the Technology Reinvestment Project. To date, the project has benefited from U.S.$1.2 million through cash, in-kind services, equipment and communications cost provided by Black & Decker (U.S.) Inc., the University and three federal government agencies. The project demonstrates three features:

1. Migration from one videoconferencing technology to another: Started in 1994 with funding from the National Defense Conversion Act, the project initially served Black & Decker employees using the corporate interactive video link. Now it also uses desktop videoconferencing. Operating on one telephone line in the point-to-point desktop mode, the Creative Labs Inc. software runs on a 486 computer and modem. The software package provided to students includes equipment such as a camera; the only other requirement is a standard analog (not digital) telephone line. Multipoint capability is expected shortly.
2. Site flexibility: Students can study at their workplace, in either a group setting using a corporate video link or at their desk, or at home.
3. Social and economic benefits: The project's practice-based Master of Science is designed to serve defense industry scientists and engineers affected by defense industry downsizing and military base closings.

The project's director, Dr. Barry DuVall, reports that international partnerships are a growing focus of activity. "Our goal is to offer courses anywhere in the world. We already do serve students who have been deployed to Greece and Korea." Dr. DuVall also notes that the technology offers greater control to students. "The beauty of the technology is that it enables students to put together programs from institutions anywhere in the world."

> We find that more and more businesses have access to the Internet. Our future course offerings may therefore make less use of desktop videoconferencing than at present, because the software we use now requires everyone to be on-line at the same time. We plan to use the Internet more because its asynchronous features are more attractive to our learners, who tend to be busy executives.
>
> *Dr. Barry DuVall,*
> *Technology Reinvestment Project*

DO MINORITY CULTURES AND SPECIAL NEEDS LEARNERS USE THIS APPROACH?

Serving Special Needs Learners through Desktop Video Learning

Stakeholders in Saskatchewan and Ontario

This six-month project was designed to assess the benefits of desktop videoconferencing equipment in providing educational opportunities to students with severe disabilities. The project demonstrates that Video Learning can fill specialized niches and that a critical mass of users can be created by developing a geographically dispersed consortium of users that cuts across schools, colleges and the private sector.

Partners in the project were the Saskatoon Board of Education, the Saskatoon Catholic Board of Education, the Peel Board of Education, the Dufferin-Peel Roman Catholic Separate School Board, Erinoak (an institution providing habilitation/rehabilitation and support services to children and young adults with

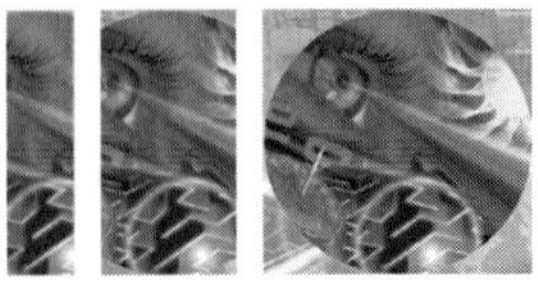

"AN EXTENDED START-UP TIME IS NEEDED FOR A PROJECT OF THIS SIZE AND DISTRIBUTION. WE DID NOT ANTICIPATE VERY ACCURATELY THE COMPLEXITY OF STARTING THE PROJECT. ONE OF THE RESULTS WAS THAT SITES CAME ON-LINE OVER A PERIOD OF WEEKS, WHICH LIMITED THE NUMBER OF SESSIONS WHICH WE WERE ABLE TO ORGANIZE." (SUSAN ALCORN MACKAY, DIRECTOR, SPECIAL NEEDS REGIONAL RESOURCE CENTRE, CAMBRIAN COLLEGE)

physical disabilities who live in the Peel and Halton regions of southern Ontario), Nipissing University in North Bay, Ontario, and Cambrian College of Applied Arts and Technology in Sudbury, Ontario. Figure 4.10 shows the geographic distribution of the partners.

A total of 12 institutions, 10 of which were elementary or secondary schools, took part in the project, although each particular application involved point-to-point videoconferences. The level of activity was high: Cambrian College, for example, participated in approximately 60 sessions over the six-month period ending in April 1995.

Two Stentor Alliance members, SaskTel and Bell Ontario, and ADCOM Inc. were the technical partners. ADCOM made 10 two-line desktop videoconferencing units available for the trial, while Bell and SaskTel provided long-distance service and technical support. Cost information is not available.

Four application areas were tried, with an interesting range of results. The first application was sign language instruction. The two-line mode worked well for signed conversation among the hearing-impaired participants, but the delay impeded effective instruction in signing techniques. Participants who experimented with the equipment felt that the six-line mode would have been needed for teaching purposes. As a result of this finding, a planned sign language instruction module did not occur.

Quadriplegic students with cerebral palsy in Sudbury and Saskatchewan were linked for peer support and sharing sessions once or twice a week for a total of 30 to 40 sessions. Ages ranged from 12 to 45. These sessions were designed to overcome the isolation that many students felt at being "the only

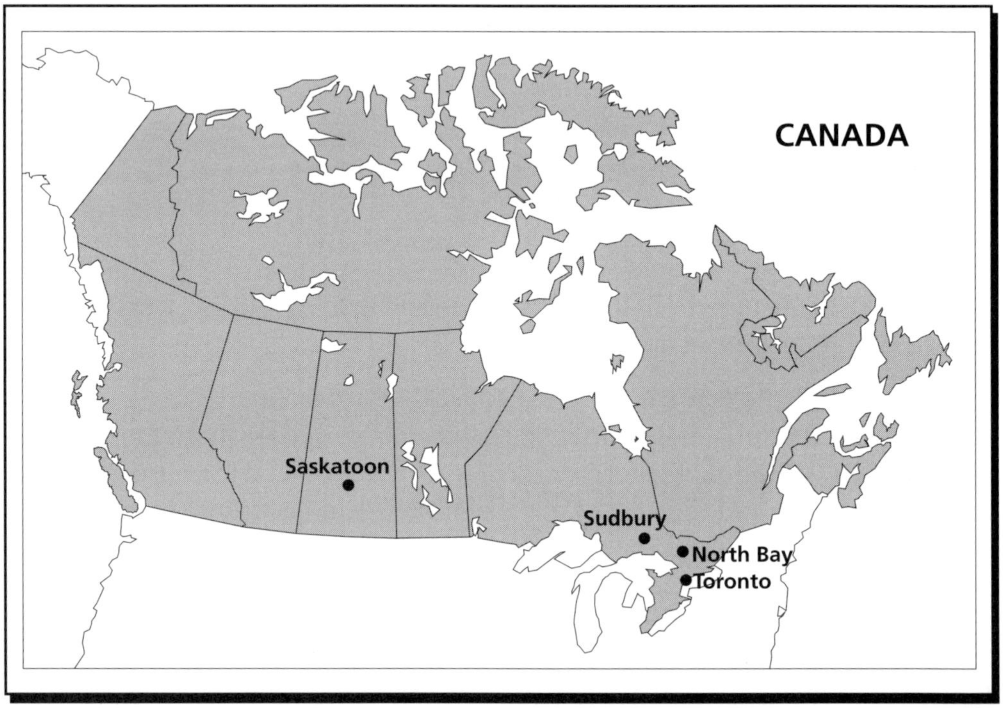

FIGURE 4.10: Geographic location of partners in the Special Needs Project

one" in their community. Most sessions involved only one or two people at each site. "The opportunity to share hopes, dreams and frustrations with others sharing the same physical and mental limitations was very important for the six students who participated," reports Susan Alcorn MacKay, the director of the Special Needs Regional Resource Centre, Cambrian College.

YOU MAY WANT TO TRY THE TWO-LINE CLASSROOM MODE YOURSELF. TAFE IN AUSTRALIA RUNS A COURSE IN THE TWO-LINE MODE EVERY SECOND SEMESTER THAT TEACHES AN INTERPRETATION LEVEL COURSE IN SIGN LANGUAGE.

Young people with developmental disabilities also engaged in peer support sessions, in which a whole class at one site was linked with one or two learners at another site.

Susan taught a special needs course for teachers-in-training at Nipissing University, a Northern Ontario institution that had its own videoconferencing equipment. This 36-hour course, Foundations in Exceptionalities, was part of a B.Ed. program. One of the advantages of using videoconferencing was that specialized software and assistive devices for those with special needs and their teachers could be demonstrated during the course by both Susan (as the instructor) and the participants at the University.

Unfortunately, the partners were not able to purchase or retain the equipment after the six-month trial, and so the momentum generated was somewhat lost. However, many of the schools involved in the project tested applications other than those related to special needs, and in this way the project created a degree of broadly based interest that had not been part of the initial project design.

> We in the Stentor Resource Centre and our school partners concluded that videoconferencing has a place in urban schools, because it facilitates access to experts anywhere in the world who would otherwise never come into schools, even those in highly urbanized areas such as the Halton and Peel boards.
>
> *Ron Klassen, Market Manager, Signature Service Centre, Stentor Resource Centre Inc.*

"THE MOST IMPORTANT THING WE LEARNED WAS THAT DOING SOMETHING NEW TAKES TIME—TIME FOR THE TECHNICAL INSTALLATION, TIME FOR TEACHERS TO 'PLAY WITH THE EQUIPMENT' SO THAT THEY KNOW HOW TO DEVELOP APPLICATIONS FOR IT, AND TIME TO FIND PROGRAM COLLABORATORS IN OTHER INSTITUTIONS." (ROLF POLAN, MARIAN M. GRAHAM COLLEGIATE INSTITUTE (SK))

Serving Aboriginal Learners through the Virtual Institution Model

KAYAS Cultural College, High Level, Alberta

On January 7, 1994, the Little Red River Cree Nation Board of Education in High Level, Alberta, created KAYAS Cultural College to provide training to the people of the Little Red River Cree Nation and to offer programs to those wishing to study the unique culture of Canada's First Nations. This initiative illustrates how new educational institutions can be created without having to build buildings and is an example of how Video Learning approaches are empowering aboriginal peoples to acquire culturally appropriate education.

> Our Elders have always stressed, especially in today's world, that our culture and language are very important and that they must be kept and protected: that is who we are as a people. But the Elders also say it is important to get an education. To have true self-government, we must be prepared the best way possible. We must understand other cultures and learn to work with them and still be our own people. We have found that we can have the best education and still be in our own communities with our language and culture, by using videoconferencing.
>
> *Rita Loonskin, former Director, KAYAS Cultural College*

The College uses Video Learning to deliver quality education to adults in three remote northern Alberta communities that comprise the Little Red River Cree Nation (see Figure 4.11). Of the three communities, only one has year-round road access; their total population is fewer than 3,000 people. A fourth videoconferencing unit is located at Fairview College in High Level, Alberta.

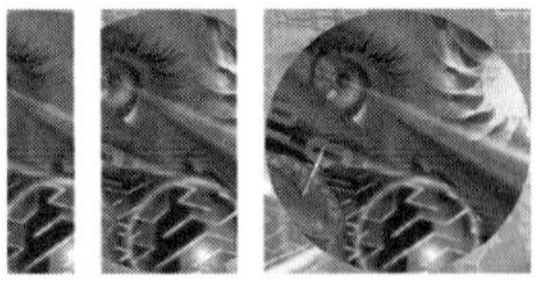

THERE IS NO IDEAL SIZE FOR A CLASS THAT IS USING VIDEO LEARNING. DUE TO THE INTENSE AND IN-DEPTH NATURE OF KAYAS PROGRAMMING, CLASS SIZES ARE RESTRICTED, BUT NUMBERS VARY DEPENDING ON THE COURSE. THIS APPROACH PROVIDES FOR MORE PERSONALIZED INSTRUCTION AND MORE INTIMATE DISCUSSIONS.

The College purchased four videoconferencing units, as well as a multipoint bridge. The equipment generally operates in the two-line mode and has been installed in existing community facilities such as the local laundromat. KAYAS is reported to be the first videoconference-based college in Western Canada and the first college in the Western Hemisphere to deliver programming using videoconferencing technology to such remote locations. Videoconferencing technology was chosen as the only cost-effective method of bringing learning resources to the three communities; face-to-face instructional costs were too high because of the communities' isolation and small populations. For example, it cost approximately Can$200,000 to deliver a 12-month Teacher Assistant Program using videoconferencing, compared with Can$550,000 to $750,000 if classroom techniques had been used.

The curriculum is initially focused on the University Transfer Program (the University of Alberta in Edmonton), the University College Entrance Program, the Teacher Assistant Certificate and High School Adult Upgrading. Future plans include credit courses in Advanced Native Studies (courses in Conversational Cree, Cree Syllabics and Native Studies) and Small Business and Accounting.

In addition to being used to distribute these formal educational activities, the videoconferencing equipment is also used for a growing number of other purposes, for example, elementary school teachers in the three communities

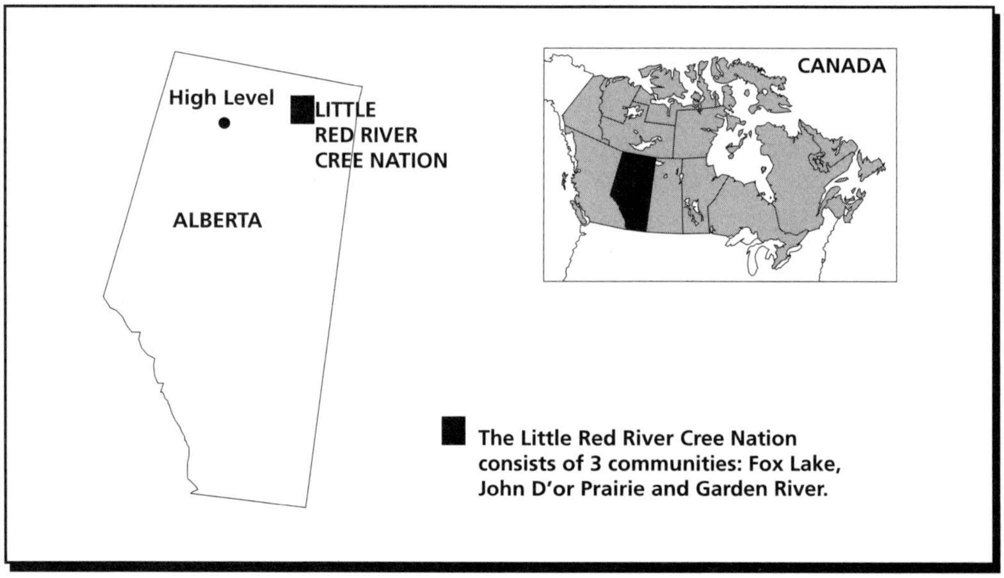

FIGURE 4.11: KAYAS videoconference locations

meet weekly to discuss their teaching plans and ideas. Also, community groups can use the system on the weekend. One example is the church committee groups from each community, who sometimes meet to discuss fund-raising activities.

International cultural exchange sessions have been held with aboriginal networks such as the Tanami Network in Australia. As described by Australian researcher Colin Latchem (1995), this network emphasizes access and privacy in conducting community, ceremonial and family business, and it has become an important means of maintaining traditional law, knowledge and social frameworks, as well as a cost-effective and culturally appropriate way of providing education and telemedicine. "The [Cree] Nation was very excited about seeing and talking to the other aboriginal people and hearing about their daily life, their struggles and successes. We look forward to other cultural exchanges in future," reports Rita Loonskin.

The College is built on a foundation of sharing, for such is the "Cree Way." Instructors work in teams of two or more, with experts from the Little Red River Cree Nation and university-accredited instructors on each team. Native peoples, particularly the Elders, are the lead instructors for Advanced Native Studies. "The academic integrity of each course is maintained by the accredited instructors working in concert with our resident experts," notes Rita.

The use of Video Learning is believed to be improving attendance rates, as well as saving money. Attendance for the various programs currently runs at 80 to 90 percent, and students have been achieving good grades. In March 1995, the College's first graduation ceremony honored 15 students who had completed the 12-month Teacher Assistant Program.

Serving the Needs of Francophone Learners

Stakeholders in Ontario and Nova Scotia

French-language virtual colleges in Nova Scotia and Ontario exemplify two different ways in which minority group institutions can use videoconferencing in collaboration with other users. The issue of the affordability of technology is particularly acute when the critical mass of potential users is, by definition, a small one.

Le Collège de l'Acadie (Nova Scotia) and Le Collège des Grands Lacs (Ontario) are single-mode distance education colleges. Distributed conferencing technologies such as video and audiographic conferencing are used to link groups of learners from the Acadian and Franco-Ontarian minority populations of these two provinces. Neither has a formal "main campus" as such; each has an administrative center and a network of learning or access centers. Faculty members are located at any of these sites or may be at totally different locations external to the college.

Both colleges collaborate closely with other networks in their respective provinces. Le Collège de l'Acadie works closely with Network Nova Scotia

(NNS), which is the responsibility of the Nova Scotia Educational Communications Agency. Created to provide an electronic infrastructure to improve access to lifelong learning, NNS is a "network of networks" over which Nova Scotia colleges, universities, schools, other institutions and businesses can offer learning through audiographic conferencing facilities. The Collège is a partner in this network and thus benefits from advantages such as (1) access to sites other than its own seven-point videoconferencing/audiographic network and (2) the special educational tariff offered by the province's telephone company to NNS.

Le Collège des Grands Lacs is part of a consortium of dual-mode, French-language postsecondary institutions in Ontario, the Franco-Ontarian Distance Education Network. This network has several goals such as (1) to improve access to postsecondary education for Franco-Ontarians, (2) to enhance the regular programs that each French-language institution already offers and (3) to offer a variety of basic programs through the exchange of live, real-time courses. The network considers videoconferencing to be a key technology linking its classroom sites (see Figure 2.2) across the province of Ontario. Initially consisting of five sites, it is expanding to 26 sites. Both networks use the two-line mode as their standard.

Recognizing that mass media can foster an environment where a majority culture overwhelms a minority one, Francophone distance educators across Canada have found that distance education technologies (especially the interactive, network-based technologies such as videoconferencing) are a means to preserve and enhance their cultural identity. One key factor is the collective critical mass that can be created through the use of technology to justify the cost of developing and offering courses. The other key factor is that a minority can share videoconferencing costs with the majority as long as the Francophones have control of the content.

CONCLUSION

This chapter has described 15 examples of the successful use of Video Learning in a wide variety of settings: in mature organizations and in consortia that are in a formative stage; in the public and private sectors; and in Canada, Europe and Australia. Each has been chosen to relate to points made elsewhere in Parts 1 or 3. For reasons of space and convenience, there is not a "one-to-one" match, point by point. Information is provided at the end of the book to enable you to contact those whom we interviewed if you want more detail.

These examples will have served their purpose if they stimulate you to think about how you can adapt their experiences to yours and if you are able to cross-reference the insights of our informants to other sections of this book and the videotape.

Now that we have examined how others are using Video Learning successfully, let's examine in more detail the design, development, delivery and evaluation strategies that you can use so that you can become a successful user of Video Learning.

References

Adam, D., & Carrier, D. (1993). *Enseignement universitaire et francophonie, analyse d'une expérience potentiellement exemplaire*. Toronto and Ottawa, ON: Authors.

ADCOM Telecom Systems Group. (1995). Cree Nation establishes "Virtual College" with videoconferencing. *The inside Edge, 2*(2), p. 1.

Alcorn MacKay, S. (1995). *VIEWS Project Final Report*. Sudbury, ON: Cambrian College of Applied Arts and Technology.

Burge, E. J., & Roberts, J. M. (1998). *Classrooms with a difference: Facilitating learning on the Information Highway* (2nd ed.). Montréal, QC: Chenelière/McGraw-Hill.

Canadian Association for Distance Education (CADE). (1995, June). Cambrian College embarked on pilot project. *Communiqué*, 7.

Chugh, U. (1993). *Evaluation of a graduate videoconferencing course: Students' and instructors' perspective*. Calgary, AB: University of Calgary, Centre for Distance Learning and Innovative Technologies.

Daesler-Lohmueller, C. (1995, June). *Evaluation of a videoconferencing course at the University of Calgary*. Calgary, AB: Centre for Distance Learning and Innovative Technologies.

DuVall, J. B. (1994, December 28). The factory as a learning laboratory. *Industry Report*, p. 3.

DuVall, J. B. (1995, May). Learning at a distance. *Manufacturing Engineering Magazine*, p. 16.

Henshaw, D. M., & Balch, D. (1995, June). Distance learning and telemedicine in rural North Carolina – technology network for a better tomorrow. In D. Sewart (Ed.), *One world, many voices: Quality in open and distance learning* (pp. 108-111, Vol. 1). Selected papers from the 17th World Conference of the International Council for Distance Education, Birmingham, United Kingdom.

Huron County Board of Education. (n.d.). *Videoconferencing opportunities and partnerships*. Clinton, ON: Author.

The Distance Education Network Project. (1995). In Knowledge Connection Corporation, *Technology and learning: Innovative projects in Ontario in 1995* (p.151). Prepared by N. McKinnon, A. Stahmer, & L. Green. Toronto, ON: Author.

La création d'un réseau d'enseignement par vidéo interactif en Ontario français. (1995, automne). *Connexion, 6*(5), 7.

Latchem, C. (1995). See what I mean? Where compressed digital conferencing works. In F. Lockwood (Ed.), *Open and distance learning today* (pp. 98-107). London, UK: Routledge.

Lamy, T., (1995). *Videocommunication: A faculty guide to learning and communicating by compressed videoconferencing* (J. Roberts, Trans.). Sudbury, ON: Laurentian University, Centre for Continuing Education. Aussi disponible en français.

MacDonald, D. (1998). *Audio and audiographic learning: The cornerstone of the Information Highway*. Montréal, QC: Chenelière/McGraw-Hill.

Ontario Learning and Technology Exchange Consortium (OLTEC). (1995, August). *Evaluation report on joint pilot project for delivery of interactive, video distance education and training courses*. Prepared by OLTEC Technology Committee, C. David Sadleir, Chair. Toronto, ON: University of Toronto, Faculty of Applied Sciences and Engineering.

Pearson, R., Freeman, W., Lederman, E., Richmond, J. M., & Thomasos, G. (1995). *Videolink Project. Final Report – Draft*. Toronto, ON: Addiction Research Foundation.

Pearson, R., & Freeman, W. (1995, May). *Taking videoconferencing for a test-drive*. Presentation at the Association for Media, Technology and Education in Canada Conference, Guelph, ON.

Pearson, R., & Freeman, W. (1997, February). *Educational technologist as change agent: Lessons learned from four innovative development projects*. Presentation at the Association for Education, Communication and Technology, Albuquerque, NM.

Rettinger, L. A. (n.d.). *Desktop videoconferencing: Technology and use for remote seminar delivery*. Unpublished master's thesis, North Carolina University. Available: http://www2.ncsu.edu/eos/service/ece/project/succeed_info/larettin/thesis/

Roberts, J. M., & Sowa, W. (1995, June). Knowledge exchange and distance education: Ontario Learning and Technology Exchange Consortium. In D. Sewart (Ed.), *One world, many voices: Quality in open and distance learning* (pp. 149-152, Vol. 1). Selected papers from the 17th World Conference of the International Council for Distance Education, Birmingham, United Kingdom.

Stahmer, A., & Green, L. (1995). CIBC develops a learning organization. *The Training Technology Monitor, 2*(6), p. 1.

Thomas, N. A., & McDonell, D. (1995). The role(s) of technology in minority group distance learning. In J. M. Roberts & E. M. Keough, *Why the Information Highway? Lessons from open & distance learning* (pp.185-199). Toronto, ON: Trifolium Books Inc.

Transport Canada, Training Directorate. (1993, October). *Videoconferencing technology as a medium for distance learning*. Ottawa, ON: Author.

Van der Perre, G., Van den Branden, J., & Van Heddegem, J. (1994, June). EuroPACE 2000, a pan-European telematics network activated by universities and their partners in learning. *Industry and Higher Education, 8*(2), 90-96.

Van der Perre, G., Van den Branden, J., Van Heddegem, J., & Ketels, M. (1995). EuroPACE 2000: Professional and academic channel for Europe 2000. In D. Sewart (Ed.), *One world, many voices: Quality in open and distance learning* (pp. 179-181, Vol. 1). Selected papers from the 17th World Conference of the International Council for Distance Education, Birmingham, United Kingdom.

Van der Perre, G., De Witte, K., Van den Branden, J., & Van Heddegem, J. (in press). Continuing education and training: Response of higher education. In R. Balcon (Ed.), *Comett final evaluation report*. Brussels: European Commission, DG XXII.

PART 3

HOW CAN I USE COMPRESSED VIDEO LEARNING SUCCESSFULLY?

Part 3 guides you in the planning, delivery and evaluation of Video Learning. Chapter 5 highlights selected active learning principles that enhance success and underlines the need for learner support systems. Chapter 6 indicates the importance of having a learning designer as a partner for instructors as they prepare the print, visual and verbal elements of Video Learning sessions. Chapter 7 tackles the problematic issue of how many people "should" be in a session and then gives you the opportunity to learn about 10 different types of instructional formats that have already been used successfully to facilitate Video Learning. Chapter 8, the book's final chapter, describes evaluation issues and presents key research results for your consideration.

Chapter 5

What Active Learning Principles Should I Use?

Compressed videoconferencing is a relatively new addition to the instructor's toolbox. Using this tool in old ways fails to maximize its potential. Strategies that promote active learners are the key to success. Passive learners with instructor-centered lectures and talking heads are not what's needed. Both instructors and students should be focused on acting in ways that promote interaction with content and with one another... ways that result in learning.

CHERE CAMPBELL GIBSON,
UNIVERSITY OF WISCONSIN—MADISON,
MADISON, WISCONSIN

INTRODUCTION

An essential premise of this book is that learner needs and styles should drive the application of learning using videoconferencing equipment, not vice versa. In this chapter you will find out more about the learning principles that have been briefly touched upon in previous chapters, and you will be introduced to the topic of learner support systems.

WHAT LEARNING PRINCIPLES ARE CRITICAL TO SUCCESS?

Active Learning

Practitioners and researchers find that, for learning to take place, learners should be able to exert some control over the learning process. In other words, they should be able to exercise a degree of real power. For example, to achieve maximum success, Liz Burge and Judy Roberts (1993, 1998), co-authors of another book in this Series, suggest that adult learners should be involved in finalizing the learning objectives that relate to their needs and to what they know already. While the degree of control will be affected by factors such as the age of the learner and the setting in which the learning takes place, the principle is nonetheless a very important one.

> ... we must put users [learners] at the center of the learning [training] process, but not leave them there alone...
>
> Author's translation of Barchebath & Lajus, 1993

Active Learning in Video Learning

Television, like other information or communications technologies used to facilitate learning and job performance, challenges the learner's ability to influence the learning process. Initially, television was designed to be watched and "consumed" by the viewing public at large or by a specific group in a "closed-circuit" environment. Educational television functioned in its early days on a "mass media" model, which left the learner/viewer isolated before the television set, powerless to intervene or participate in the program.

More recently, educators have developed many successful techniques to promote interaction in broadcast environments. However, Video Learning allows learners to participate in and control their learning even more readily than they do with interactive broadcasts. New behaviors for learning are being formulated that release both instructors and learners from the conventional television viewing mentality. Such behaviors, which are described throughout Parts 2 and 3 of this book, are designed to capitalize on well-established principles of how our active and passive behaviors affect how much we retain from a learning activity.

TABLE 5.1: HOW MUCH WE RETAIN FROM A LEARNING ACTIVITY

WE RETAIN
10 percent of what we READ
20 percent of what we HEAR
30 percent of what we SEE
50 percent of what we HEAR and SEE
80 percent of what we DO
90 percent of what we SAY and DO

Source: Centre de recherche informatique de Montréal (CRIM), 1992.

Since feeling that one can act is a necessary precondition for actually acting, learners and instructors need to become partners in developing and implementing active "Video Learning behaviors" that are distinct from passive "broadcast television behaviors."

To maximize the interactive learning and performance support potential of the technology, Part 3 examines questions such as:

- How do we adapt our behavior to the new type of television language, attitudes, rhythms and behaviors made possible in Video Learning? (Chapter 6)
- How can we develop a communication process between instructor and learners that maximizes effective learning? (Chapter 7)
- How can we encourage learners to discard their passivity and control their own learning through Video Learning? (Chapter 8)

If we do not, as instructors, model and encourage new behavior, students reportedly revert to passive behavior, listen haphazardly and ignore the visual picture on the television screen, according to learning designers such as Margaret Haughey (1993) at the University of Alberta in Edmonton.

Videocommunication

This book answers these questions by recommending specific teaching and learning activities that are based on principles of communication (intentional exchange and communion) and interaction. These practical suggestions are derived from a philosophy that can be briefly articulated as follows: With Video Learning, we enter into what a colleague, Thérèse Lamy (1995) from Montréal, Québec, describes as a process of videocommunication, not television viewing. She believes that videocommunication calls for a unique visual and audio protocol that can only be implemented by abandoning the passive broadcast television mode. New learning and teaching approaches must be, and are being, developed that are adapted to the new technology's characteristics and to the power that it can give to the learner.

These approaches can be based on existing classroom or distance education knowledge. For example, Virginia Ostendorf (1994), a consultant in Littleton, Colorado, notes the work Thomas Cyrs and Frank Smith (1990) have done at New Mexico State University on the importance of asking good questions. They rank questions on a scale measuring those that require the least sophisticated thinking to answer and those that demand the most. Using an appropriate mix of questions will contribute to the learning that occurs in a session regardless of the technology used.

In Video Learning, as in other forms of communication for learning and performance support, we should create an environment that leads to "moments of communication," when learners exchange various points of view generated by their experience, life history and knowledge. Learning thus becomes a process of exchange among participants who believe in mutual respect and reciprocal enrichment. The teaching/learning process is a shared experience, with effects as unanticipated as those of a kaleidoscope.

Your role as an instructor or learning facilitator is to permit two essential types of activities to take place. The first is to enable participants to acquire self-confidence, to identify and value what they already know, and to express it. The second is to put in place communication protocols adapted to the participants' needs and to the program's learning and performance objectives. Let's now return to critical practical considerations related to implementing this philosophy.

WHAT ARE LEARNER SUPPORT SYSTEMS?

We are still at an early stage in understanding how learner characteristics affect the outcome of Video Learning. Based on research results and practical experience with other technologies, we can expect that learner characteristics such as age, gender and culture, as well as the type of support services offered by the institution, will affect how quickly students become active video learners. The term applied to the study and application of these factors is "student support systems." Here are some examples of the practical issues that have emerged from the use of other technologies:

1. Women seem to need more interaction during learning than men.
2. On-site or remote tutors should be provided to coach and mentor students as they complete assignments.

3. Good library resources are required both on-site and in remote areas.
4. Academic, career and personal counseling services may be required, especially if students need to acquire or refresh study and exam writing skills.

Jane Brindley, a psychologist and distance education consultant in Sudbury, Ontario, believes that "instructors should not be asked to address these issues by themselves. A wide range of skills and services are required to support the development of active learners. As the person present in the classroom, the instructor can become a vital link to librarians, school counselors and other relevant support services. Such a multidisciplinary team approach can accelerate the process of developing active learners."

In addition to consulting the references cited in this chapter, we recommend that you pursue some of the Further Readings listed for Chapter 6.

CONCLUSION

Video Learning works best with active learners who have a sense of control over their learning and over the technology. In this chapter you have learned why we believe this to be true, and you have been introduced to the concept of videocommunication as a learner-driven process, facilitated by instructors who know how to use Video Learning to create appropriate environments. You have also reviewed the critical role learner support systems play in enabling learners to be successful in Video Learning. In Chapter 6 you will learn how to prepare for your Video Learning session in ways that build on these principles.

References

Barchebath, E., & Ponts-Lajus, S. (1993). L'interactivité sociale au risque de la technologie. *MSCOPE*, 5, 62-67.

Burge, E. J., & Roberts, J. M. (1998). *Classrooms with a difference: Facilitating learning on the Information Highway* (2nd ed.). Montréal, QC: Chenelière/McGraw-Hill.

Centre de recherche informatique de Montréal (CRIM). (1992). *Les environments informatisés de formation: Synthèse de la consultation de la littérature*. Montréal, QC: Author.

Cyrs, T. E., & Smith, F. (1990). *Teleclass teaching: A resource guide* (2nd ed.). Las Cruces, NM: New Mexico State University.

Haughey, M. (1993, October). *The University of Alberta and Alberta Transportation and Utilities Videoconferencing Project, 1992-93*. An evaluation report. Edmonton, AB: University of Alberta.

Lamy, T. (1995). *Videocommunication: A faculty guide to learning and communicating by compressed videoconferencing* (J. Roberts, Trans.). Sudbury, ON: Laurentian University: Centre for Continuing Education. Aussi disponible en français.

Ostendorf, V. A. (1994). *The two-way video classroom. Edition for PictureTelearning*. Littleton, CO: Author.

Chapter 6

How Do I Prepare for Video Learning?

One of our biggest challenges was to convince people that there are right and wrong ways to use the technology and that training [of both instructors and learners] was the way to bridge the gap.

TELEMEDICINE/TETRA TEAM,
MEMORIAL UNIVERSITY, ST. JOHN'S,
NEWFOUNDLAND AND LABRADOR

INTRODUCTION

In this chapter you will discover how a learning design professional can assist you in preparing for your Video Learning session. You will consider four areas of preparation necessary for effective videocommunication: print support, visual learning materials, verbal techniques and combining the verbal and visual elements. You will conclude with a review of general presentation issues and using the equipment.

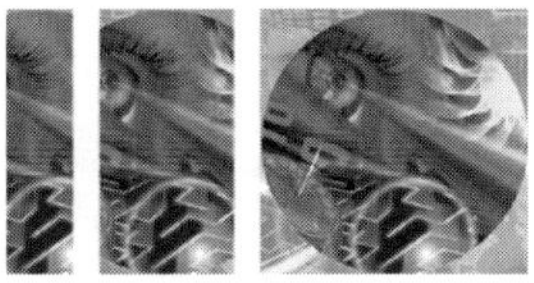

EACH OF THESE ISSUES WILL BE PRESENTED SEPARATELY, BUT IT IS A GOOD IDEA FOR YOU TO CONSIDER THEM AS A GROUP. AT THE OUTSET, MAKE A LIST OF ALL THE TASKS THAT NEED TO BE COMPLETED. THE CRITICAL PATH PROCESS IS AN EXCELLENT FORMAT TO USE IF YOU ARE FAMILIAR WITH IT. BE ORGANIZED!

WHY IS A LEARNING DESIGNER AN IMPORTANT PARTNER?

Conceptualizing and organizing a course that uses Video Learning requires us to take multiple factors into account: learning objectives, content characteristics, the skills to be developed, the teaching model, learners' emotional needs, the teaching materials to be used and communication dynamics. When these elements are integrated effectively, we create videocommunication.

As an instructor, you will generally have help in preparing your materials. One key helper is the instructional or learning designer. This person works with instructors to design courses or workshops and is an expert in understanding how to integrate learner characteristics with theories and practice about how learning occurs, as well as with the strengths and weaknesses of various technologies. The learning designer may also integrate the efforts of graphic artists, videotape producers and other professionals who may contribute to your session depending on how complex it is and what resources are available. Caroline Gray in the Learning Systems Group at the CIBC is a learning designer, for example.

An alternative approach taken by some institutions is to train instructors to perform many of these functions themselves. We believe, however, that a designer is enormously useful and would argue that an instructor's primary responsibility in designing a course should focus on content, not learning design. However, we also believe that, even if the services of a designer are available, the instructor should understand some of the fundamental issues

REVIEW THIS LIST WITH THE OTHER MEMBERS OF YOUR TEAM. DETERMINE WHICH OF THE FUNCTIONS ARE RELEVANT TO YOUR SITUATION, AND DECIDE WHO IS RESPONSIBLE FOR EACH TASK.

about preparing quality print and visual materials in order to be an effective member of the team. The balance of the chapter will give you tools that will enable you to collaborate with a designer.

The following is a planning checklist developed by Transport Canada. We hope you will find it useful as you continue your reading.

TABLE 6.1: TRANSPORT CANADA PLANNING CHECKLIST

- ☑ Assess learner needs of target population.
- ☑ Set objectives.
- ☑ Confirm that videoconferencing is the optimum method of delivery for all or portions of the course.
- ☑ Develop or amend lesson plans and evaluation strategies.
- ☑ Advise guest presenters (let them know that videoconferencing will be used).
- ☑ Recruit and train far-end site facilitator(s) as required.
- ☑ Establish participant list and notify participants.
- ☑ Confirm time, location(s) and dial-up videoconference numbers (remember to account for different time zones).
- ☑ Book rooms and request flip chart or other aids and equipment as required.
- ☑ Contact participants and confirm time and place.
- ☑ Distribute agenda/course outline to all participants.
- ☑ Prepare all course documents in advance.
- ☑ Prepare graphics for display on the document camera.
- ☑ Mail/fax course materials in advance and confirm arrival of materials prior to meeting.
- ☑ Have a contingency plan in mind.
- ☑ Establish rules and guidelines for the session.
- ☑ Review all audio-visuals and audio-graphics.
- ☑ Rehearse your presentation.
- ☑ On the day of the videoconference, plan to set up room and camera angles 30 minutes before the session begins.

Source: Transport Canada, Training Directorate, 1993, p.17.

WILL I NEED PRINT SUPPORT MATERIALS?

Two types of print support materials are needed: (1) a Learner's Guide and (2) a textbook.

A print Learner's Guide is required for Video Learning courses and training events. This is a communications tool that helps the learner navigate through the session. It may be a simple, fairly short document for a half-day training event or a more elaborate publication for a semester-long course. Samples are provided in Liz Burge and Judy Roberts' (1998) book in this Series.

USERS SUCH AS THE CIBC REPORT THAT PRINT MATERIAL WAS ESSENTIAL—EVEN FOR A SHORT TWO-HOUR OR THREE-HOUR TRAINING EVENT. (CAROLINE GRAY, CIBC LEARNING SYSTEMS GROUP)

In the formal education system, this document is generally called a study guide, course syllabus or course outline. Prepared by the instructor, a study guide resembles a course description, except that it is much more elaborate. For example, you should consider including a note that welcomes the participants to your session, a list of everyone in the course, an explanation of why Video Learning has been chosen as the learning tool, tips for active Video Learning and the names of who to contact with questions about course content, learner support systems or equipment problems. Assignments and evaluation instruments may also be included in the guide.

YOU CAN FACILITATE LEARNER ACCESS TO THE GUIDE BY MAKING IT AVAILABLE IN BOTH PAPER AND ELECTRONIC FORMATS.

We suggest that you take these two steps when developing your print support materials:

1. Plan: Choose the content, determine the objectives and the learning activities (before, during and after the videoconference) and select the evaluation tools. Determine which types of visual materials—graphics, photographs, slides or videotapes—you will use at different points in time.
2. Take action: Write the document. Order enough copies for all the participants and convert the master to an electronic format well in advance. Have any texts or documents photocopied several weeks prior to the course. Obtain copyright clearance for materials you plan to use such as written materials, videos, films, software and audiotapes.

You may also need a textbook if the learning session is long, for example, three months in duration, or if the learning objectives require a textbook and an appropriate one is available. Depending on your context, a procedures manual or a collection of memos or found articles may be used as a "textbook."

TECHNIQUES DESCRIBED IN THE BALANCE OF THIS CHAPTER ARE BASED ON MODIFYING TRADITIONAL "PRESENTATION" MODES OF LEARNING; HOWEVER, THEY CAN ALSO BE GENERALIZED TO MORE COLLABORATIVE MODES.

WHAT VISUAL PRESENTATION MATERIALS SHOULD I PREPARE?

Since most videoconferencing systems have a document camera, you can use visual learning resources such as maps, diagrams, illustrations, models and printed text during your session. These should be prepared ahead of time and tailored to the following specifications:

YOU MAY WANT TO USE THE INTERNET AS A SOURCE OF CONTENT MATERIALS.

1. Use pastel-colored paper, not white, to minimize glare.
2. Respect television's three-by-four aspect ratio. As Figure 6.1 illustrates, graphics used in videoconferencing should be extended on the horizontal axis to conform to the proportion, or aspect ratio, of a television screen.
3. Use LARGE, well-spaced characters. We recommend a minimum font size of 24 points (see Figure 6.2).
4. Don't put information near the edges; stay within the "safe area" shown in Figure 6.3. The area framed by the television camera is called the scanning area. However, since detail at the edges of the scanning area is sometimes lost, design your information to fit within the safe area—inside a border that is 10 percent smaller than the scanning area. In addition, a square border should be drawn around the scanning area to allow visuals to be framed more easily.
5. Written text should have no more than five lines and a maximum of 20 words.
6. Make a number of "message slides": e.g., 15 MINUTE BREAK or READ PLEASE (see Figure 6.4). Put them under the document camera at appropriate points in the session.

THOSE OF YOU FAMILIAR WITH DESKTOP PUBLISHING AND WORD PROCESSING MAY REALIZE THAT, IN FACT, WE ARE SAYING: " USE THE LANDSCAPE LAYOUT, NOT THE PORTRAIT! "

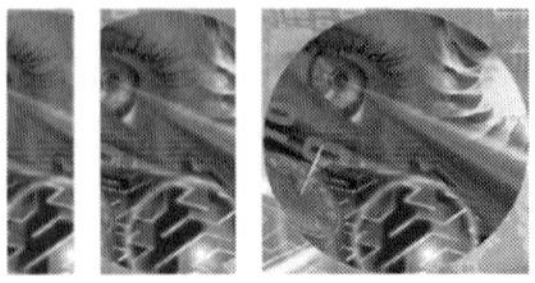

ADCOM INC., A VIDEO LEARNING EQUIPMENT VENDOR IN TORONTO, ONTARIO, RECOMMENDS THAT TO FIND OUT IF YOUR FONT SIZE IS LARGE ENOUGH, PLACE A PIECE OF PAPER WITH PRINT ON IT ON THE FLOOR. YOU SHOULD BE ABLE TO READ THE PRINT EASILY WITHOUT STOOPING OVER! (1995)

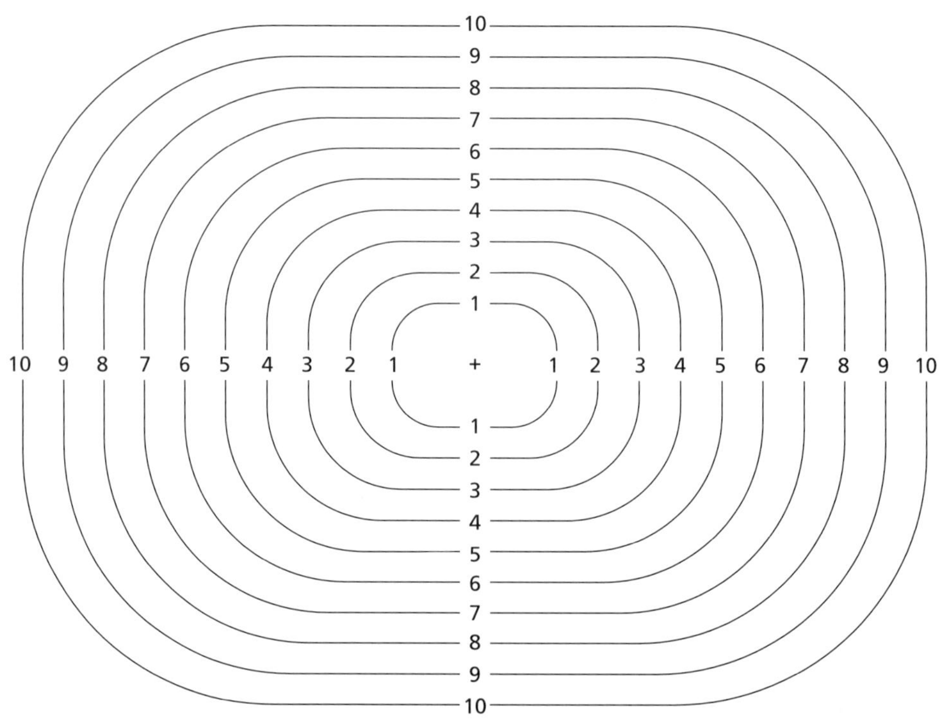

FIGURE 6.1: Aspect ratio for visual materials
Source: Hakes et al., 1993.

40 Point Font

36 Point Font

24 Point Font

18 Point Font

14 Point Font

10 Point Font

FIGURE 6.2: Sample font sizes

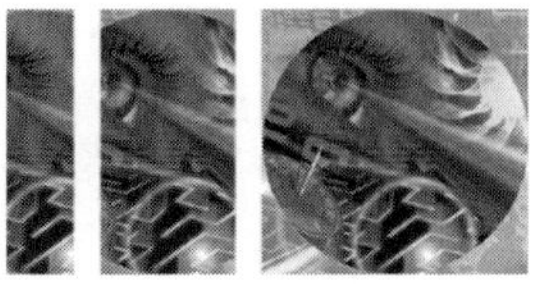

USE THE GRAPHIC IN FIGURE 6.3, WHICH IS ADAPTED FROM THE BOOK BY BARBARA HAKES AND HER COLLEAGUES (1993), AS A TRANSPARENCY TO VERIFY "WHETHER YOUR SAFE AREA IS SAFE!"

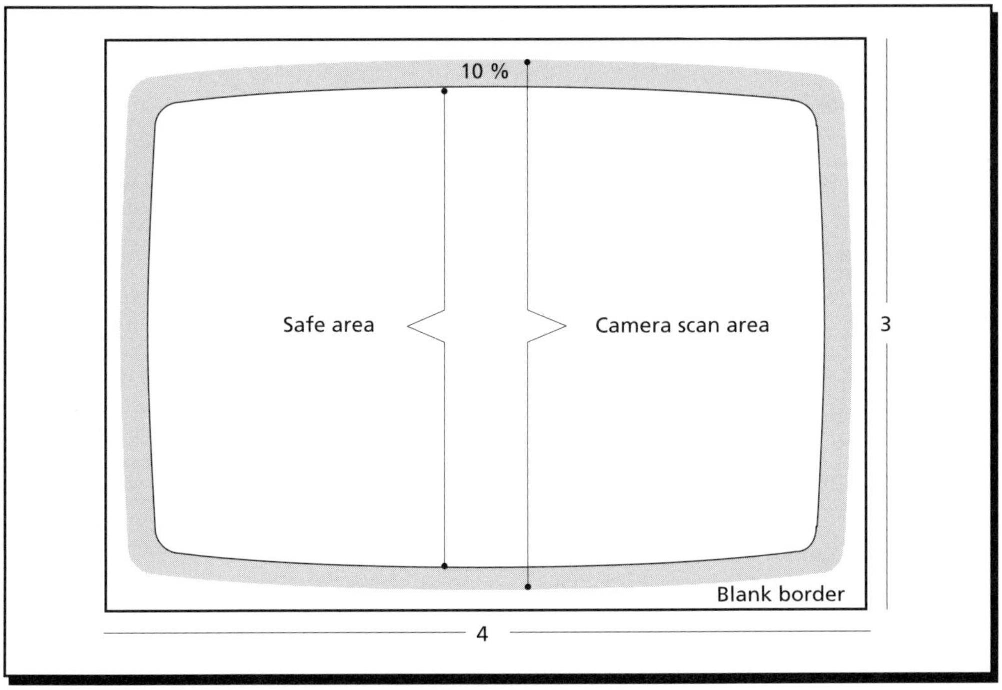

FIGURE 6.3: Template to guide preparation of visual materials
Source: Hakes et al., 1993.

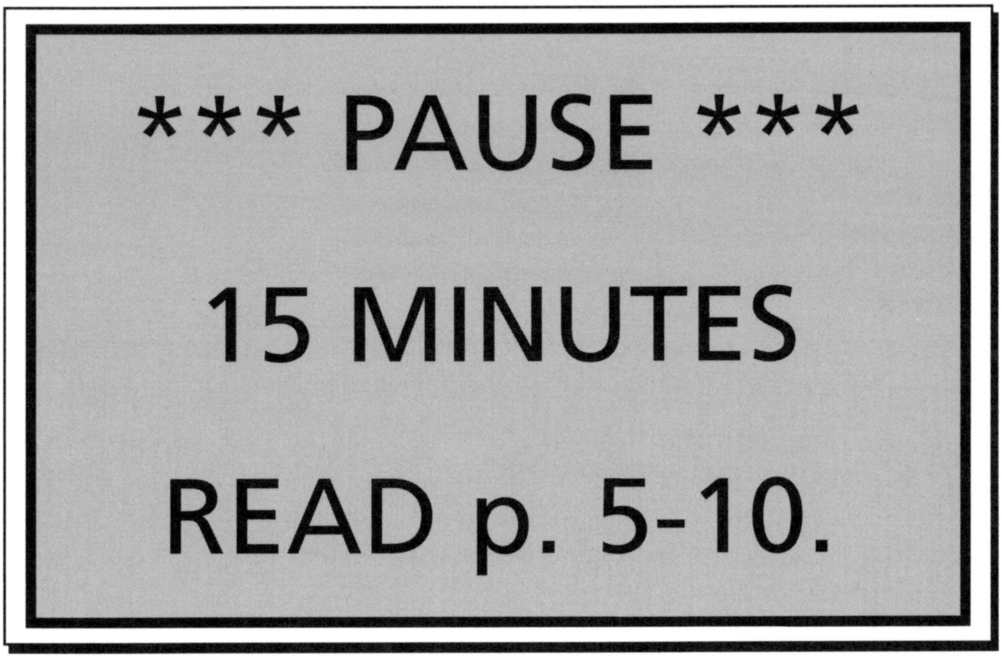

FIGURE 6.4: Sample message

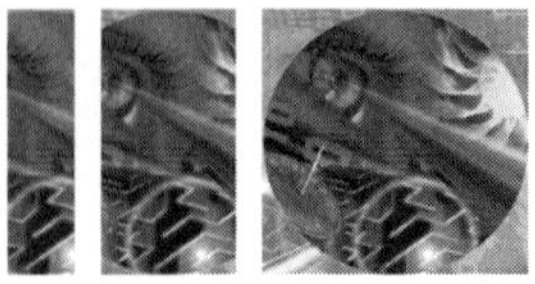

SOME OF TDC'S SUGGESTIONS ARE DIFFERENT FROM OURS. TRY BOTH AND CHOOSE THOSE THAT WORK BEST FOR YOU.

TABLE 6.2: VISUAL AIDS FOR TRANSMISSION BY VIDEOCONFERENCE

Sources

- Overhead transparencies
- Paper
- 35-mm slides
- Flip chart
- Computer graphics
- 3-dimensional objects

Preparation of Visual Aids for Document Camera

- Use a 3:4 aspect ratio – turning a $8\frac{1}{2}$ X 11 inch page on its side comes close.
- Use large text – at least an 18 point, bold typeface when displaying a lot of text; 24 to 36 point is even better.
- Use no more than 7 to 10 lines of text and no more than 30 columns of characters.
- Leave at least a $1\frac{1}{2}$ inch margin on all sides.
- Keep diagrams and charts simple.
- Blue or green characters work well; red may "bleed."
- Use a light background.

Using the Document Camera during a Videoconference

- When sending a live video graphic, do not move the image around.
- When pointing at a live video graphic, keep the pointer steady.
- When writing under the document camera
  - print with a medium or wide marker
  - keep the paper steady
  - remove your hand from under the camera after completing each item
- If you send an image as a still graphic on the second monitor
  - it cannot be pointed to or written on
  - the main video camera can still transmit images
  - a live video graphic can be transmitted simultaneously
- When finished with an image and not replacing it with another, transmit a blank image.

Source: Public Service Commission of Canada, Training and Development Canada.

Here is a checklist that covers many of these points, developed by Training and Development Canada (TDC), Government of Canada, Ottawa, Ontario. It contains some additional suggestions about how to use the document camera during the session to send materials prepared in advance, and how to write "live" during a session.

SHOULD I PAY ATTENTION TO VERBAL PRESENTATION TECHNIQUES?

While excellent print and visual support materials are important, they are not enough in themselves to create effective Video Learning. It is also important that you be easily heard and understood at all the sites so you can engage the participants.

> Worse than an instructor who has nothing to say is the instructor who takes too long to say it.
>
> Effective communication requires preparation. Improvisation leads to mediocre communication.
>
> *Thérèse Lamy (1995), a distance education and learning design consultant in Montréal, Québec*

Keep in mind the following points about preparation, volume, tone, clarity, pauses, rhythm and enthusiasm in order to be an effective videocommunicator.

PREPARATION It is useful to ask yourself questions such as, Who are the participants? What is their prior experience and knowledge of the content? Appreciating the participants' prior knowledge enables you to adjust your approach, choose an appropriate vocabulary, ask relevant questions and make references they will understand.

VOLUME Even though your voice is being transmitted by a microphone, it is important for you to project well since the microphone needs a good, clear signal. Try breathing deeply as a way to increase the level of your voice. You don't need to raise the volume too much though — the people on the screen aren't at the back of the room!

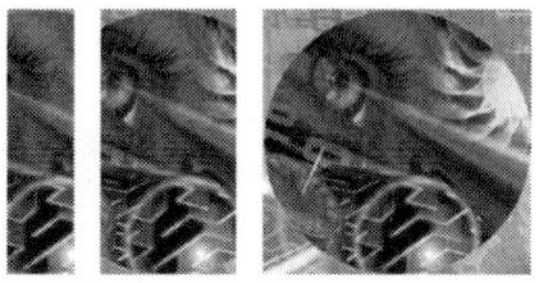

IF YOU WANT TO WORK ON THIS SKILL, MAKE A TAPE OF YOURSELF SPEAKING AND LISTEN TO HOW YOU SOUND. THE TAPE COULD ALSO FACILITATE YOUR EVALUATION OF THE VIDEOCONFERENCING SYSTEM'S AUDIO QUALITY, AN ISSUE DISCUSSED IN CHAPTER 4.

TONE Try to find a low tone you are comfortable with so your voice doesn't sound tight. Tense voices are difficult to listen to for any length of time. Breathing deeply will improve tone as well as volume.

CLARITY The quality of your verbal presentation is improved by articulating words clearly and pronouncing them correctly.

PAUSES Wait a few seconds (15 is a good target) for a reply to your question or to make a comment after someone else intervenes. The equipment is voice-switched and does not permit two people to speak simultaneously.

If you feel the clock is creating a distracting sense of "always watching the clock," count slowly in your mind to 15. Be time-aware, not time-constrained.

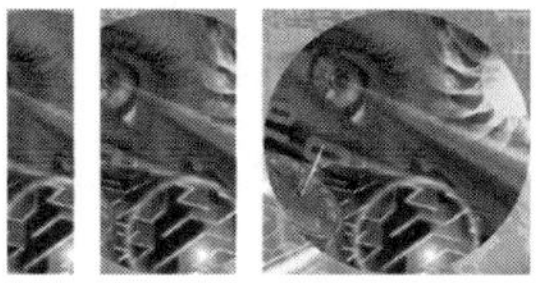

FIFTEEN SECONDS CAN SEEM LIKE A LONG TIME. TO HELP YOURSELF AND YOUR LEARNERS ACQUIRE A SENSE OF 15 SECONDS AS AN INTERVAL, USE A CLOCK WITH A SECOND HAND. IF THE ROOM DOES NOT HAVE A CLOCK WITH A SECOND HAND, BRING ONE FOR THE FIRST FEW CLASSES OR UNTIL YOU BECOME COMFORTABLE WITH THE PAUSES.

RHYTHM For many people, an electronic environment creates a fair amount of nervousness and a tendency to talk very quickly in a monotone. It is important to speak at a moderate rate and to vary both your tempo and intonation. The pace of your presentation can be varied by changing your tone of voice, by altering your body language and by using pauses, questions and illustrations.

You should alter the pace of your presentation according to the reactions you see among participants. When you are teaching in the point-to-point mode, it is easy to see everyone's reactions. However, when Video Learning is multipoint, reactions are more difficult to see as there is only one television monitor switching among the sites. Therefore, when preparing your session, it is important to develop a plan that varies both pace and rhythm. You could, for example:

1. limit the number of concepts presented

2. present each concept completely and illustrate it with examples
3. make linkages among the concepts
4. anchor new concepts in previous ones
5. make linkages with other parts of the course or with events in the workplace

ENTHUSIASM If the subject or teaching process bores you, you can be sure the participants are bored as well. Enthusiasm and passion for the subject matter are contagious, especially in videocommunication.

HOW DO I COMBINE VISUAL AND VERBAL PRESENTATION MATERIALS EFFECTIVELY?

To retain learners' involvement, it is critical that both the visual and verbal elements of the presentation are effective and that each conforms to the guidelines discussed in previous sections: to prepare documents and visuals appropriately, to use different types of media during a session and to use effective verbal techniques. Equally important, however, is the way in which the visual and verbal elements are combined. We recommend that you focus on duration, synchronization, competition and conflict, coherence and pertinence when deciding how best to combine the various elements of your presentation.

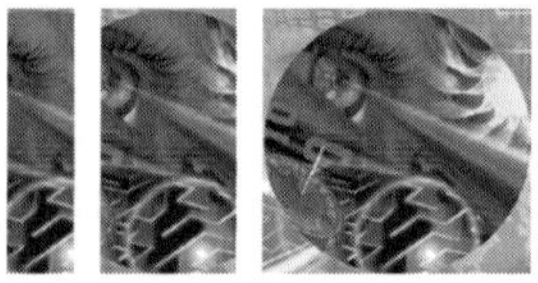

KEEP THE MATERIALS ORGANIZED IN THE SEQUENCE IN WHICH YOU WILL USE THEM SO THAT THE MICROPHONES DO NOT TRANSMIT THE SOUND OF YOU OR THE PARTICIPANTS FLIPPING BACK AND FORTH BETWEEN SECTIONS IN THE PRINT MATERIAL.

DURATION No verbal segment should be more than 15 minutes long. There is abundant evidence that interactive technologies such as videoconferencing are poor conveyers of factual information and that print is the more appropriate technology to use when information transmission is the primary goal. Resist the temptation to give lectures.

SYNCHRONIZATION Visual aids and documents should be synchronized appropriately with the content and flow of the verbal presentation.

COMPETITION AND CONFLICT The print materials should reinforce and supplement the verbal segments throughout the entire session. Conflicting inputs will impede effective learning.

COHERENCE The session should not give the impression that different bits of material were pulled together at random just to have a variety of documents.

PERTINENCE Every document that is used should make a unique contribution to attaining the session's objectives.

WHAT GENERAL PRESENTATION TECHNIQUES COULD I USE?

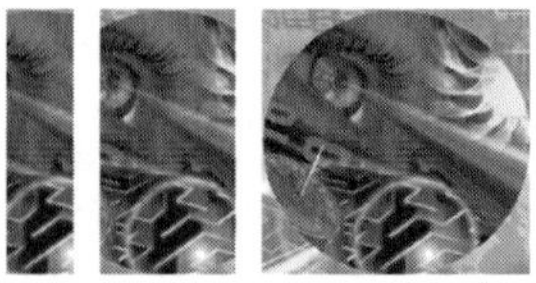

THE GENERAL POINTS LISTED HERE APPLY TO ALL THE LEARNING ACTIVITIES DESCRIBED IN CHAPTER 7.

How you animate or facilitate Video Learning sessions, how you use the camera and how you dress during a session can affect the quality of videocommunication that takes place. Here are some more ideas that describe how you can adapt your behavior to the new type of television language made possible in Video Learning.

Animation

To create a sense of presence at a distance and encourage active learning, we recommend that you welcome the participants at the outset and give them some clear guidelines describing how you plan to facilitate the session. Throughout the session you should:

1. refer to and reinforce the session's structure, underline its meaning, summarize and emphasize
2. recognize emotions (emotional reactions)
3. call upon participants to speak, either individually by name or as a group by site
4. encourage and support interaction from each of the sites

Camera Techniques

1. If no one is with you at your site, look straight into the camera rather than at the television monitor so that the participants at the other sites feel you are "looking at them" when you talk.
2. If participants are with you at your site, try to look straight into the camera as much as possible so that those at remote sites feel included. Depending on how the room is laid out, you may find it challenging to share your eye contact with both the camera and those in the room, but it is vital to establish a sense of shared presence. Some instructors prefer to be alone so that they can focus on the needs of their remote learners.
3. Avoid waving your hands as you speak. Mannerisms such as this are distracting.
4. Don't move too quickly. When only two phone lines are used, the movement will come across as jerky.
5. Don't move too far away from the camera into the corners of the room. The camera will not follow you, and it may be unsettling for others not to see you.
6. Try to vary the camera shots. Medium-angle shots, concentrated on one person, and group shots are appropriate. Very wide-angle shots can be useful, but don't use them too often as participants could become frustrated by the poor resolution in such pictures.

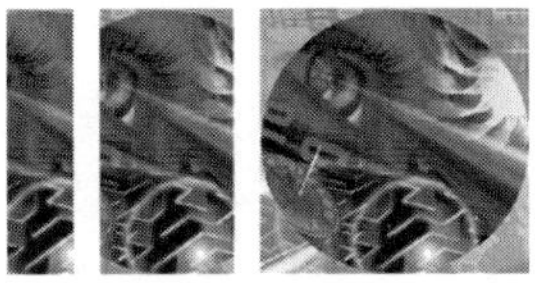

YOU MAY FIND THAT YOU NEED TO REMIND LEARNERS TO LOOK AT THE CAMERA WHEN THEY SPEAK, SO THAT EVERYONE FEELS A PART OF THE GROUP.

Clothing

1. Avoid bright, glittery jewelry, striped or bulky clothes and solid colors such as white, black and red.
2. Wear pastel colors, not bold ones, as they are easier to look at.
3. If you wear glasses, avoid tinted lenses, as they tend to create a "raccoon" look!

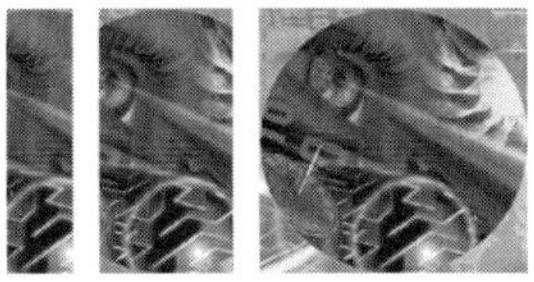

USING THE "PRE-SET" FUNCTIONS OF THE EQUIPMENT CAN AVOID CONFUSION DURING THE CLASS.

WHAT SHOULD I KNOW ABOUT USING THE EQUIPMENT?

Since you, as the instructor, will probably be the person in the session to whom learners will look for help, include equipment preparation tasks on your "to do"

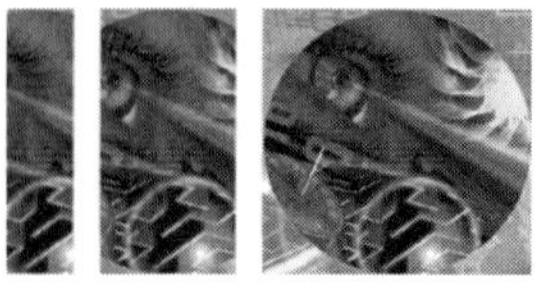

DON'T WORRY IF YOU DON'T FEEL COMFORTABLE RIGHT AWAY WITH ALL THE SYSTEM'S OPTIONS AND WITH ITS POTENTIAL. AS YOU BECOME MORE FAMILIAR WITH IT, YOU WILL USE MORE OF ITS FEATURES.

list or critical path.

1. Double-check that all the room and equipment bookings have been made.
2. Try out the equipment. We recommend that, after you participate in a videoconference demonstration, you spend a few hours familiarizing yourself with the equipment and the room setup. You could, as Sandra Hodder did, use this time to prepare or test your visual materials (see p. 44).
3. When you feel more confident, experiment with the technical systems the equipment offers such as the graphics tablet, the electronic board or computer, the graphics camera or the videotape transmission feature.

John Mitchell (1995), a videoconferencing consultant to a broad range of universities, hospitals, school systems, corporations and governments in Australia, goes even further:

> I tell instructors that it will take them 25 to 30 hours to become competent users. This includes six hours of attendance at basic and advanced methodology courses that we conduct; six hours of practice with the keypad, the document camera and other peripheral equipment; and up to 13 to 18 hours of actual use during which they are wearing their "Learner Driver" certificate.

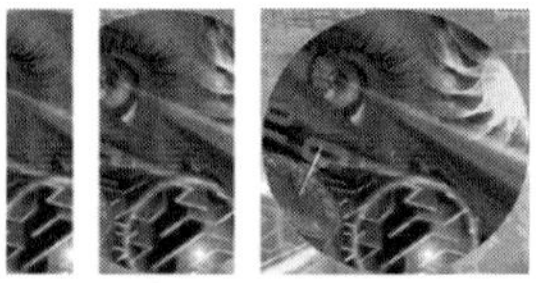

"... WHEN INSTRUCTORS FIRST BEGIN TO USE THE TECHNOLOGY, THEY SHOULD KEEP THINGS SIMPLE." (TRANSPORT CANADA, 1993, P. 15)

You might take the course before you start preparing any materials, practice at appropriate points during the preparation phase and then "jump in" to actual use.

As some of the stories in Part 2 indicate, other practitioners do not agree with John's time frame. We tend to share his views, and we draw your attention to them because you may find them reassuring if you do not learn as quickly as you think you should. John would urge you not to worry, as a long learning curve is normal and advisable.

CONCLUSION

You have now had the opportunity to consider how a learning designer can assist you in preparing for your Video Learning session. You have examined four types of critical preparation the two of you would collaborate on: print support, visual learning materials, verbal techniques and combining the verbal and visual elements. In the next chapter you will review several instructional formats that could be incorporated into your design and delivery. All of them will benefit from what you learned in this chapter about general presentation techniques and preparing to use the equipment.

References

ADCOM Telecom Systems Group. (1995, February). Conferencing tips. *The inside Edge, 2*(2), 2.

Burge, E. J., & Roberts, J. M. (1998). *Classrooms with a difference: Facilitating learning on the Information Highway* (2nd ed.). Montréal, QC: Chenelière/McGraw-Hill.

Hakes, B. T., Sachs, S. G., Box, J., & Couchenour, J. (1993). *Compressed video: Operations and applications.* Washington, DC: The Association for Educational Communications and Technology.

Lamy, T., (1995). *Videocommunication: A faculty guide to learning and communicating by compressed videoconferencing* (J. Roberts, Trans.). Sudbury, ON: Laurentian University: Centre for Continuing Education. Aussi disponible en français.

Transport Canada, Training Directorate. (1993, October). *Videoconferencing technology as a medium for distance learning.* Ottawa, ON: Author.

Chapter 7

How Do I Facilitate Video Learning?

The primary design change being made, based on participant feedback, is to give participants more opportunity for interaction and reduce the proportion of time spent in delivering content.

CAROLINE GRAY,
FORMERLY OF CIBC LEARNING SYSTEMS GROUP,
TORONTO, ONTARIO

INTRODUCTION

In this chapter you will learn about the characteristics of 10 different types of well-known instructional formats and learning activities that have been used successfully to facilitate Video Learning. These techniques offer, to varying degrees, opportunities for dialogue and interaction. How you combine them in an individual session, and how you use them throughout a series of sessions, is one of your key decisions. First, however, let's review the issue of how many participants "should" be in a session.

HOW MANY PEOPLE SHOULD BE IN A SESSION?

This issue is often raised. There may be no ideal number, but the total number of people across all sites, as well as their distribution among the sites, will affect your implementation of the generic learning formats described in this section. Three examples illustrate what we mean.

1. If a total of 100 people are distributed fairly evenly among 10 sites, you could use formats that require considerable group activity at each site and expect that each individual will have opportunities to participate. Much of that interaction could be off-line. However, when the group is in a plenary session, each individual will not be able to participate to the same degree as they would in off-line work.

2. If a total of 55 people are distributed between two sites such that one site has 50 people and the other has five, you could create five subgroups at the larger site and one at the other. You could permit the five people at the smaller site to be part of a subgroup at the larger site, as those five may need variety if several sessions are involved.

3. If a total of 15 people are registered at eight sites, with only one or two at each site, then you could make extensive use of interactive plenary formats since interaction among 15 people can occur fairly freely. Off-line, small-group work would be impractical.

Interaction in a Video Learning session is affected by numbers in much the same way as classroom interaction. If there are 100 people, there will be a lot less interaction then if there are 10 people. And, regardless of numbers, if you solicit and create interaction, there will be more questions than if you lecture a lot.

The number of people in the room also affects the clarity with which you will be able to see faces and recognize people. While the close-up feature of the camera addresses this issue, Craig Scott, a law professor at the University of Toronto who taught a course linking students in Singapore and Toronto in the winter of 1997, reports that learners in his class exchanged photographs by mail so that they could put faces to names during the Video Learning sessions.

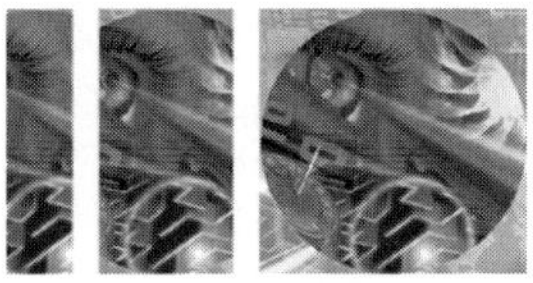

THIS TECHNIQUE ALSO WORKS WELL IN AUDIO AND NETWORKED LEARNING.

WHAT TYPES OF LEARNING ACTIVITIES ARE APPROPRIATE TO VIDEO LEARNING?

Video Learning employs many of the same formats used in the classroom or with other learning technologies. There are no formats that are unique to Video Learning. What is unique is how the availability of moving video can enrich the formats compared with when they are used in Audio Learning, or how the real-time nature of the interaction will affect the design compared with the delayed interaction experienced in Networked Learning.

To arrive at a final design, therefore, you will probably need to review Chapters 6 and 7 together and develop a learning package appropriate to your learners and content.

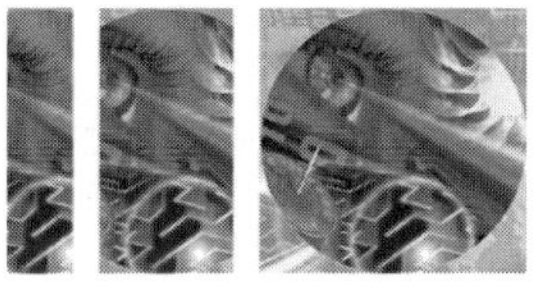

UNLESS SOMEONE ON YOUR TEAM HAS HAD MULTIPOINT EXPERIENCE, TRY THESE OUT FIRST IN THE POINT-TO-POINT MODE.

Each of the following 10 formats is described with respect to its purpose, general format, strengths and limitations.

The 10 formats include:

1. formal presentations, or lectures
2. informal presentations, or tutorials
3. seminars
4. role playing
5. problem solving
6. case studies
7. brainstorming
8. constructing content
9. simulations
10. research

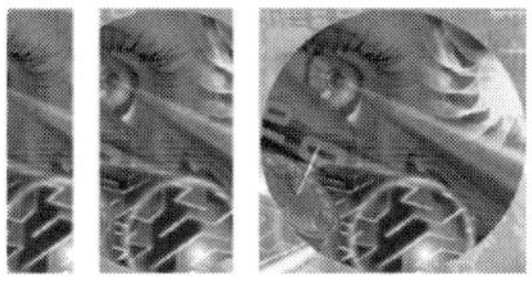

ARE YOU COMFORTABLE USING SOME OF THE MORE INTERACTIVE FORMATS THAT FOLLOW? YOU WILL NOTE THAT THE LECTURE IS ONLY ONE OF SEVERAL APPROACHES WE DESCRIBE. OUR IMPLICIT MESSAGE: BE PREPARED TO ADD NEW TECHNIQUES TO YOUR PORTFOLIO SO THAT YOU FACILITATE LEARNING AS EFFECTIVELY AS POSSIBLE.

We caution you that our material highlights the generic features of each format and should be considered as a starting point, not a destination. You will find it helpful to ask yourself how you would modify our "typical format" for different numbers and distributions of learners, and how you would vary your application of these formats for short or long education or training sequences. Space is sometimes left for you to add your own notes.

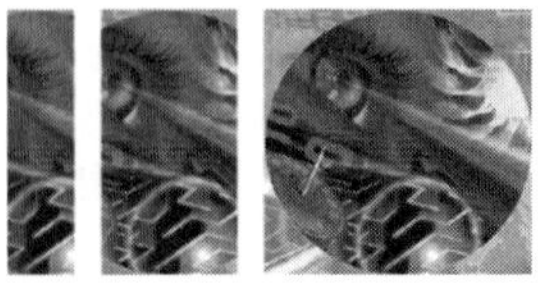

WHEN USING THE LECTURE FORMAT, ENSURE THAT NO ONE, NOT THE INSTRUCTOR OR ANY OF THE LEARNERS, TALKS FOR MORE THAN 10 TO 15 MINUTES AT A TIME. FIGURE 4.1 (SEE P. 33) IS AN EXCELLENT EXAMPLE OF HOW A "LECTURE" HAS BEEN DIVIDED INTO CHUNKS OF VARIED ACTIVITIES.

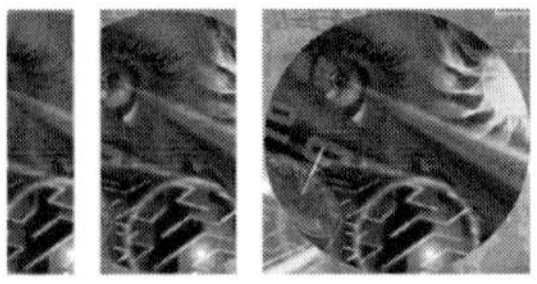

TO STIMULATE INTERACTION, POSE QUESTIONS TO SPECIFIC PEOPLE OR SITES. ASKING A GENERAL QUESTION SUCH AS "DOES ANYONE HAVE A COMMENT?" TENDS TO PRODUCE SILENCE.

TABLE 7.1: FORMAL PRESENTATIONS – LECTURES

FEATURE	DESCRIPTION
Purpose	To present or summarize information.
Format	This is typically a one-way presentation where the instructor or a guest lecturer presents "factual" content and monopolizes the session. Ideally, learners engage in intense intellectual activity and are actively reflecting about the content of the instructor's presentation. Time is set aside for participants' questions every 15 to 20 minutes, but only a few people have the opportunity to ask questions. Formal presentations can accommodate large groups of learners who are part of a plenary session and have limited expectations regarding interaction. Examples of the use of formal presentations in a videoconference include: an uninterrupted extended lecture, a series of mini-presentations interspersed with questions, inclusion of a guest speaker with appropriate Q & A sessions, and/or a demonstration.
Strengths	This format suits learners who listen well and think abstractly, and instructors who are exceptional communicators. It can be useful when introducing a set of activities, summarizing content or giving instructions. The lecture format usually requires fewer supporting materials than other formats. It is flexible and can be modified or changed by the presenter fairly easily. Learners acquire valuable listening skills. An inspirational teacher or guest lecturer can share his/her passion for the subject and generate learner enthusiasm and motivation.
Limitations	Learner initiative and collaboration are not generally stimulated by a lecture. Very few instructors can establish a climate appropriate for learning by resisting the temptation to lecture for the entire session. Students can find it difficult to interrupt or ask questions once a lecture is under way.

NOTES:

TABLE 7.2: INFORMAL PRESENTATIONS – TUTORIALS

FEATURE	DESCRIPTION
Purpose	To facilitate collaborative sharing of information among learners and instructor.
Format	This technique, like the previous one, is based upon an instructor's or guest lecturer's verbal presentation. However, in this format, the instructor and participants share the opportunity to initiate communication. The instructor's role is to set objectives, lay out content, and act as animator (facilitator). She or he interprets or comments on participants' questions and manages dialogue. Participants are free to interrupt the presentation, pose questions, make comments, suggest supplementary explanations and initiate other themes.
Strengths	Informal presentations permit two-way feedback between the participants and the instructor, thus enabling the session to be adapted to learner needs. Informal sessions encourage communication among the participants, which breaks down the sense of isolation and anonymity and creates a feeling of belonging. Participants learn from one another, not just from the instructor. This format also facilitates the creation of knowledge if learners prepare ahead of time through activities suggested in the study guide, such as reading, watching a videotape or engaging in laboratory activities.
Limitations	The instructor has to be very flexible in order to adapt quickly to changing circumstances. As with the formal presentation, this format favors auditory learners more than visual learners, and those who function at an abstract, rather than a concrete, level. Gaps can, however, be filled if additional visual elements or relevant individual assignments are given.

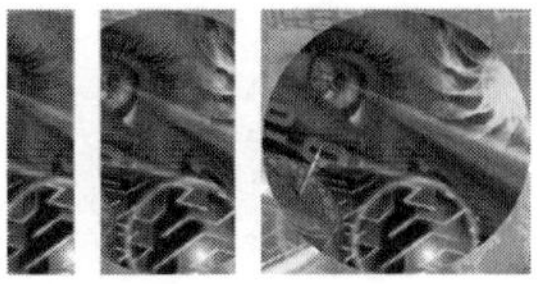

VIRGINIA OSTENDORF (1994), A VIDEO LEARNING CONSULTANT IN LITTLETON, COLORADO, RECOMMENDS THAT AN INSTRUCTOR TRACK, BY MEANS OF THE CLASS LIST, THE FREQUENCY OF PARTICIPATION BY ALL INDIVIDUALS IN EACH SESSION. SUCH A FORMAL "PAPER TRAIL" IS USEFUL IN DETERMINING WHO IS MONOPOLIZING THE INTERACTION TIME AND IN SELECTING THOSE WHO NEED TO BE ENCOURAGED TO INTERVENE.

NOTES:

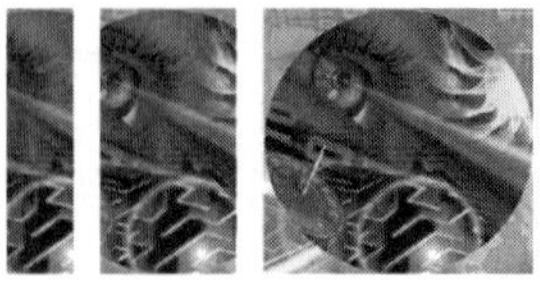

OUR COMMENTS ON PAGES 82-83 ABOUT HOW TO DIVIDE PARTICIPATION DEPENDING ON THE NUMBER OF LEARNERS AT EACH SITE ARE PARTICULARLY PERTINENT TO THIS FORMAT.

TABLE 7.3: SEMINARS

FEATURE	DESCRIPTION
Purpose	To learn how to conduct research on an assigned topic. To learn how to structure content for effective communication by respecting certain precise guidelines.
Format	Before the videoconference, participants conduct individual or group research and prepare necessary visual materials such as overhead transparencies, printed handouts, computer slides and videotapes. During the session, each participant makes a presentation within an agreed time limit and responds to questions from the group. The instructor has a twofold role: information provider and moderator. As information provider, she or he ensures that, throughout the seminar, content is pertinent. As moderator, she or he ensures participation and fair play among the participants and generally facilitates the discussion. Since a large part of the seminar is the verbal interaction and exchanges among the participants, it is critical that they prepare well during the preconference activities assigned in the study guide.
Strengths	The seminar format exploits the group's resources and maximizes everyone's performance because of the exchanges, or dialogue. This format links people and encourages the development of personal relationships. By facilitating active participation by everyone, a seminar can develop the learners' sense of autonomy and independence. The latter point is a crucial one: in distance education, as in all learning, learners need to take charge of managing their learning.
Limitations	Certain instructors find it difficult to relinquish their role as presenter and to function as a facilitator. Moreover, sometimes the participants themselves put pressure on the instructor to lecture. Preparing learners for the seminar format is essential for success and for meeting the challenge of creating effective dialogue.

Figures 4.4 to 4.6 from the Bell/ARF Videolink Project are a good example of seminar formats.

NOTES:

TABLE 7.4: Role Playing

FEATURE	DESCRIPTION
Purpose	To motivate participants to examine their own experiences to find the elements required by their role and by the assigned content.
Format	Role playing consists of an improvised scene between two or more players (students) who work to guidelines given by the instructor (who has sketched a minimum amount of detail regarding the situation). After hearing the scenario in an opening plenary, learners divide into pairs or small groups. Each person interprets their role without having previously learned any script; all words and actions are spontaneous. After a set time period for "rehearsal," each pair or group presents their interpretation of the assigned roles. The presentations are normally followed by a review (debriefing, analysis) of the substance and process, a step that does not occur in other forms of simulation.
Strengths	This format can be a particularly lively form of videocommunication once participants learn to become spontaneous. It is very flexible, as many situations lend themselves to role playing. In addition to acquiring communication skills, participants generally come to better understand the motivation of those they are emulating and become more aware of social and psychological problems. A variation of the simulation format, it emphasizes affective learning and encourages spontaneity and empathy.
Limitations	Role playing is not appropriate for several types of learning objectives. It does not, for example, facilitate the transmission of a lot of content or factual material. It is best used only by instructors who feel very comfortable with the role of animator. It is difficult to retain and use what has been learned/occurred in role playing unless a videotape is made. If the room has to be rearranged, only limited changes or rearrangements may be possible because of videoconferencing's characteristics.

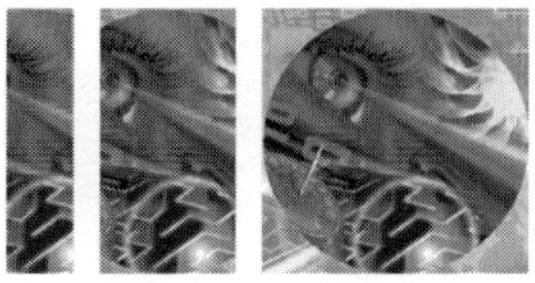

Craig Scott, a law professor at the University of Toronto, who taught a course by Video Learning for the first time in the winter of 1997, used this format at the start of his cross-cultural course between Singapore and Toronto to introduce the students to one another and to relax them by having some fun. He found this technique particularly useful because one goal of the course was to teach the students how to put themselves in someone else's shoes. However, he found it best to limit its role to that of initial "ice-breaker"; otherwise, the students' engagement was constrained by their ability to hide behind roles.

NOTES:

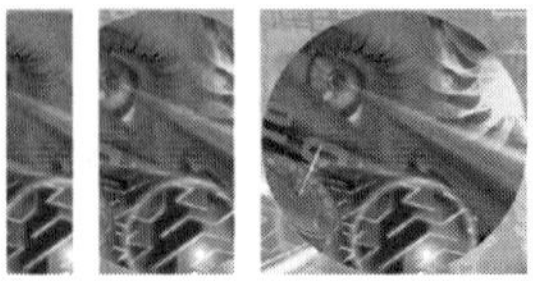

IF AN EXPERIENCED FACILITATOR IS AVAILABLE AT EACH SITE, THE TIME REQUIRED FOR GROUP WORK CAN BE SHORTER THAN IF EACH GROUP HAS TO WORK THROUGH ITS PROCESS ISSUES UNAIDED. EVEN EXPERIENCED LEARNERS LIKE TO START WITH SOME STRUCTURE.

TABLE 7.5: PROBLEM SOLVING

FEATURE	DESCRIPTION
Purpose	To learn how to use one's own knowledge and experience, as well as relevant elements, to solve a problem and/or improve job performance. To learn how to observe and to enrich one's own knowledge from the knowledge and experience of others. To develop an independent attitude toward specialists so that they complement, not dominate, one's knowledge.
Format	This activity involves an initial presentation of information by the instructor or a guest expert to the group, followed by a challenge to learners that they create a synthesis of the primary information and come up with hypothetical solutions. They typically do this in a small-group format and then report back in a plenary session. The instructor or guest lecturer may conclude the session with a few thoughts about the points raised by the small-group presentations. It is a learning activity that lends itself to groups of a limited size at each site, for example, five to eight people.
Strengths	It is a format that assumes everyone's participation, enhances mutual learning and facilitates group work (working in teams). It permits the achievement of a variety of pedagogical objectives in both the cognitive and affective domains. It increases the likelihood that the students will develop a sense of initiative and autonomy.
Limitations	This format requires, from both the instructor and the learners, a certain level of experience in group dynamics. Many participants feel a high level of insecurity in a setting that leaves so much room for individual initiative and for shared activity (working with others).

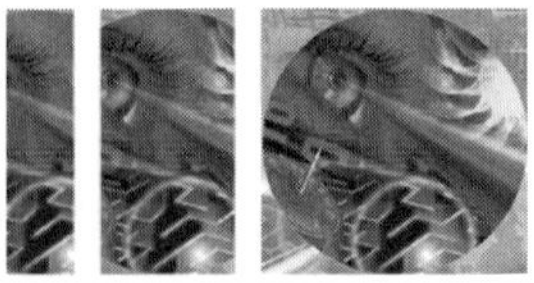

IF YOU PLAN TO RELY HEAVILY ON FORMATS SUCH AS CASE STUDIES AND PROBLEM SOLVING, DEVOTE TIME TO DISCUSSING THE PROCESS WITH THE LEARNERS BEFORE ASSIGNING THE CONTENT. AGREE IN ADVANCE ON HOW LONG EACH PHASE WILL TAKE AND HOW CONTROVERSY WILL BE HANDLED. SUCH AN INVESTMENT OF TIME WILL PAY OFF IN THE QUALITY OF INTERACTION.

TABLE 7.6: CASE STUDIES

FEATURE	DESCRIPTION
Purpose	To analyze problems that are based on real situations.
Format	Using resources such as a prerecorded videotape or written reports, the instructor describes as briefly as possible a case drawn from real life. In addition to being readily summarized, case studies should emphasize one point in particular. The plenary group then divides into small groups to develop a situation analysis, a technique necessary to understand the situation precisely. The general rules, ideas or concepts that could apply to other similar situations are identified. Finally, if possible, a solution is sought to the problem. After this small-group work, the plenary is reconvened and each group presents its findings.
Strengths	It is an excellent format for training people in diagnosing and resolving human problems. It permits the application of theoretical knowledge to concrete situations. Exchanges among participants are a key component of the exercise and are easy to encourage.
Limitations	Preparing good case studies takes a lot of time for an instructor. The training value of this format may be weak the first time it is used, as participants may need time to learn to function in their small groups. Planners should either allocate a generous amount of time to the session or plan to use several case studies. Its success depends on the group members' ability to work together and the instructor's ability to prepare appropriate material to stimulate the small groups and facilitate a reporting process that involves all sites.

TABLE 7.7: BRAINSTORMING

FEATURE	DESCRIPTION
Purpose	To generate a large number of original ideas in a short period of time.
Format	A situation or problem is described to the group. A time limit is indicated. The participants, in small groups, make a list of ideas without evaluating or filtering them. One person is group reporter. At the end of the time period, in a plenary discussion, all the ideas are listed. Only after they have all been listed are they evaluated by the whole group. Then a consensus is arrived at as to which would lead to the best solution.
Strengths	The format calls forth creativity from each participant and maximizes interaction. The format permits many cognitive and affective pedagogical objectives to be achieved.
Limitations	Participants may find it difficult to synthesize their thoughts after a period of divergent creativity, or they may be prone to judge ideas in the small group, thus limiting the range of ideas that are developed. The instructor should prepare strategies to deal with both possibilities.

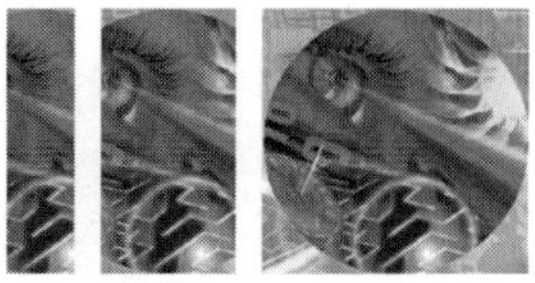

THESE TWO TECHNIQUES ARE PARTICULARLY APPEALING TO INSTRUCTORS WHOSE STYLE FOCUSES MORE ON THE LEARNERS CREATING THEIR OWN KNOWLEDGE AND LESS ON THE INSTRUCTOR IMPARTING EXISTING "RECEIVED WISDOM."

TABLE 7.8: CONSTRUCTING CONTENT

FEATURE	DESCRIPTION
Purpose	To learn how to value one's own knowledge and experiences. To enrich one's knowledge of others. To make linkages between one's own knowledge and experiences and those of others.
Format	Typically, the instructor proposes a theme (topic). The participants are invited to share what they know about the topic. The instructor takes note of the interventions, questions people, throws questions back to them and enables them to clarify their meaning. This process, if done well, permits the instructor to document precisely what students already know and to compile a list of any inaccurate information, stereotypes or prejudices related to the topic. Once the comments are finished, the instructor summarizes and validates the appropriate knowledge the group described, presents other information critical to an understanding of the subject, and corrects – in a positive way – misunderstandings that may exist within the group. Participants are then invited to express their understanding of the instructor's summary.
Strengths	This format is particularly suited to achieving intellectual objectives, while still valuing and confirming the social dimension of learning. It also inspires a sense of confidence in the participants, who generally find that they know more about a given subject than they thought they did.
Limitations	It is a very demanding process for the participants, who must engage themselves in it and defend their points of view without being close-minded about others' ideas. The instructor plays the double role of animator (who facilitates discussion) and content expert (who corrects misunderstandings, challenges prejudice and adds essential information).

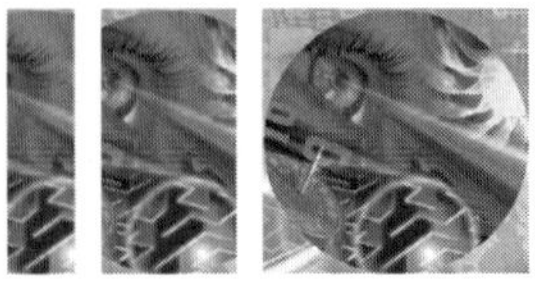

LEARNERS NEED TO BE FAIRLY COMFORTABLE WITH VIDEO LEARNING BEFORE THIS FORMAT IS USED.

TABLE 7.9: SIMULATIONS

FEATURE	DESCRIPTION
Purpose	To permit learners to confront or examine various aspects of a real situation without being in the actual situation.
Format	Participants are placed in a simulated environment in which they are asked to act as if they were in the actual situation. The instructor is both animator and content provider. A computer may be needed for many simulations. For example, the instructor could present a computer simulation of a process and show a videotape of real events on which the simulation is based. Then the students could be asked to research the phenomenon and develop different computer simulations based on different mathematical or scientific assumptions. This format is appropriate for groups with a limited number of people, say 5 to 10.
Strengths	This format permits learners to experience complex situations and problems that might be too dangerous or costly to present in any other manner. It requires a high level of interaction among the participants and readily lends itself to the integration of videoconferencing with computer and mathematical models.
Limitations	This is a very demanding format from the animation perspective. It requires a high degree of planning by the instructor and considerable preparation by the students.

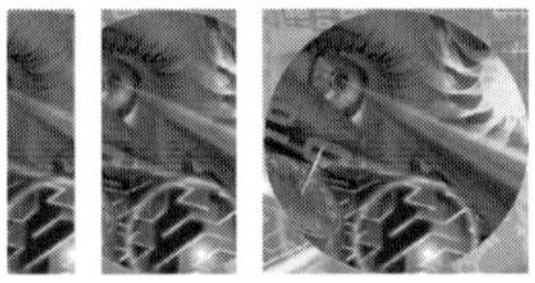

ALLOWING STUDENTS TO RESEARCH TOPICS OFF-LINE CAN BE A WAY TO BUILD THEIR CONFIDENCE ABOUT THEIR CAPACITY TO USE THE VIDEOCONFERENCING EQUIPMENT.

TABLE 7.10: RESEARCH

FEATURE	DESCRIPTION
Purpose	To learn how to observe and collect information. To learn how to enrich one's knowledge based on a concrete activity.
Format	The instructor describes a research topic with the help of illustrations (prerecorded videotapes, experts, etc.). Depending on the complexity of the topic, the assignment might be described fairly quickly at the end of the session, or be documented in some detail in a session entirely devoted to the topic. After the videoconference, the participants perform their research individually or in groups, and then, in the next session, return to share their results with the whole group. At that time, each person benefits from information presented by the others and individual knowledge acquired in the research process is expanded.
Strengths	This format permits several intellectual objectives to be attained. It allows each participant to work independently while still requiring communication with the group.
Limitations	This process can be fairly time-consuming and lengthy. This format may have fairly limited relevance in some workplace situations.

CONCLUSION

If you prepare properly when designing your course, following the suggestions made in Chapter 6, and if you choose appropriately among the 10 different learning activity formats in Chapter 7, you are well on the way to creating conditions for effective Video Learning.

Let's now consider how we might evaluate the success of our planning and delivery.

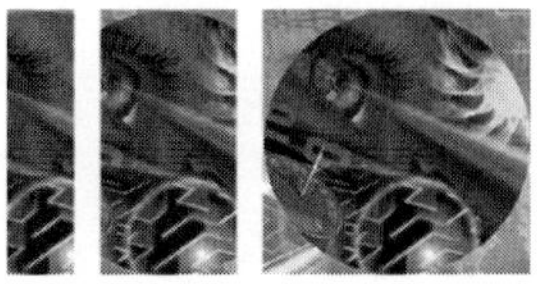

PILOT YOUR TECHNIQUES WITH SMALL NUMBERS OF SITES, IF POSSIBLE. IF SUCH AN APPROACH IS NOT PRACTICAL, DRY RUNS SHOULD BE USED BY BOTH INSTRUCTORS AND STUDENTS.

Reference

Ostendorf, V. A. (1994). *The two-way video classroom. Edition for PictureTelearning.* Littleton, CO: Author.

Chapter 8

How Do I Evaluate Video Learning?

Constant evaluation was critical to the pilot project. We developed a list of those aspects of the technology which we wished to test, created opportunities to do so, collected data continuously during the pilot and made changes as the project proceeded.

MURRAY RICHMOND,
FORMERLY OF EDUCATION & TRAINING,
ADDICTION RESEARCH FOUNDATION,
TORONTO, ONTARIO

INTRODUCTION

In this chapter you will review four levels of evaluation that could be applied to Video Learning, examine some sample evaluation instruments and consider the results of evaluations conducted to date.

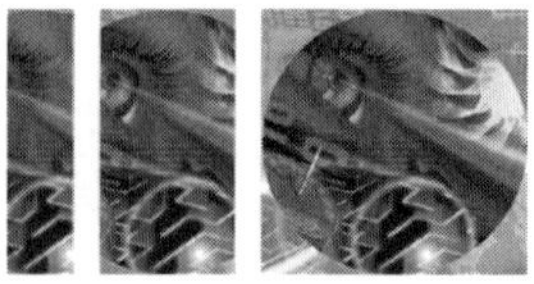

A NOTE ABOUT TERMINOLOGY, SIMILAR TO THE ONE MADE AT THE BEGINNING OF CHAPTER 1, IS RELEVANT IF YOU WANT TO FIND ADDITIONAL STUDIES. SOME TITLES DO NOT CONTAIN THE TERM *COMPRESSED VIDEOCONFERENCING*, BUT USE ALTERNATIVE TERMS SUCH AS *VIDEOCONFERENCING* OR *ISDN*. YOU MAY THEREFORE HAVE TO LEARN THE TECHNICAL TERMINOLOGY DESCRIBING COMPRESSION TECHNOLOGIES IN ORDER TO LOCATE RELEVANT LITERATURE.

WHAT LEVELS OF EVALUATION COULD I USE?

As in other evaluation contexts, there are different levels of evaluation that can apply to Video Learning. Transport Canada (1993, p. 28) uses jargon-free language in describing four types of evaluation measurements—participant reaction, learning, application and impact—that are based on the framework developed by Donald Kirkpatrick (1996) at the University of Wisconsin.

1. Participant reaction refers to the degree to which instructors, learners, administrators or other stakeholders are satisfied with their Video Learning experience.
2. Learning assessment measures the amount of content acquired and/or retained by the learners.
3. Application examines if the learners can apply the knowledge, skills or new attitudes they acquired in the videoconference to a practical setting such as their work environment.
4. Impact determines if applying their acquired knowledge, skills or attitudes makes any difference in the learners' personal or professional lives.

To date, many Video Learning evaluations, including evaluations of the projects described in Chapter 4, have focused only on participant reactions. The bulk of the results indicate that participants, both instructors and students, are satisfied with Video Learning and would use it again. Figure 8.1, the evaluation form used in the ERCnet/OLTEC trial, is a concise example of this type of evaluation. Participants in the three two-day seminars were asked to complete it after each session. A more in-depth telephone survey was conducted after the trial was over.

AUDIENCE EVALUATION FORM

The seminar in which you have just participated is the first one to use the ERCnet, linking the Universities of McMaster, Waterloo and Toronto, and their industrial partners. We would like to have your views on how effective you found this format to be, as well as your suggestions for future improvements.

(1) Your site (circle one): McMASTER WATERLOO TORONTO XEROX

Your room position (circle one): FRONT MIDDLE REAR

(2) Could you read and hear the material presented by the lecturer adequately? Please cite any specific aspects (font sizes, choice of colors, etc.) that you think could be improved.

(3) Could you interact adequately with the instructor and remote classmates? If not, please explain the difficulties.

(4) Compared with a traditional presentation in which the instructor is in the same room with the entire class, please tell us how effective you found this course, and provide any suggestions you think might improve future courses.

(5) Finally, please add any other comments you wish. Your feedback is appreciated. Thank you for taking the time to provide it.

FIGURE 8.1: Audience evaluation form

As we saw in Chapter 4, many of the people interviewed for this book felt that continuous evaluation was important to success, particularly over a series of learning sessions. Small adjustments to your video-communication process can make all the difference between success and failure as measured by user acceptance.

Learning assessment studies have firmly established that anyone can learn effectively through any type of videoconferencing. Tom Russell (1992), a practitioner at North Carolina State University in Raleigh, conducted a comprehensive review of the literature and found that there is no significant difference in learning outcomes between classroom and any type of videoconference learning. In our opinion, there is therefore very little need for studies that compare the scores obtained by learners taking a course through Video Learning with those of learners taking the same course in a classroom.

However, the literature on participants' reactions indicates that HOW one uses Video Learning is critical to the perception that learning is taking place and that the process is acceptable. We therefore suggest that you follow the advice of colleagues such as Murray Richmond, formerly at ARF, or Caroline Gray, previously at CIBC, and evaluate your Video Learning process regularly so you can modify it to meet your learners' needs. The ERCnet form, for example, could readily be adapted and used in a series of sessions to help you make adjustments based on participant feedback.

Because issues such as return on investment and performance improvement are assuming a growing strategic importance in both the public and private sectors, evaluation studies that include application and impact are needed. The case studies in this book are typical of the literature in general; none deal with applications or impact.

You may find it helpful to consult a book such as Tara Knott's *General Planning and Evaluation Guide to Distance Education* (1994). Every category that Tara, an evaluation specialist in Memphis, Tennessee, applies to "distance education" could also apply to Video Learning. You could modify some or all of the sample evaluation forms and questions that she provides.

WHAT EVALUATION INSTRUMENTS ARE APPROPRIATE?

In Appendix 1, examples are provided of evaluation instruments that are too long to reproduce in this chapter. Each serves a purpose and was useful to its creator. Deciding what your evaluation goals and needs are will help you determine what type of evaluation instrument is most suitable to your situation.

You could also adapt a form designed for another technology. Liz Burge and Judy Roberts (1998) provide examples of such forms in another book in this Series, *Classrooms with a Difference: Facilitating Learning on the Information Highway* (2nd ed.).

WHAT GUIDANCE DO CURRENT RESEARCH FINDINGS PROVIDE FOR ME?

We have based many of the suggestions in this book on the findings of evaluation studies, as well as on other sources. In Chapter 4, we reported on the impressionistic and anecdotal evaluation issues that were uppermost in the minds of our interviewees. In this section, we highlight the findings from three structured formal evaluation studies that illustrate the types of results available in the literature.

We divide the results into two subsections: (1) teaching and learning issues and (2) implementation issues.

Teaching and Learning Issues

The University of Calgary graduate engineering course discussed in Chapter 4 (see pp. 51-52) was evaluated in some depth by Ms. Urmil Chugh (1993) when she was attached to the Centre for Distance Education and Innovative Technologies. Her report describes students' and instructors' learning or teaching styles and behaviors at a level of detail not often found in evaluations that address participant reactions. Her results remind us of both the opportunities and the challenges faced in preparing and facilitating active Video Learning.

THOSE OF YOU WHO ARE PARTICULARLY INTERESTED IN RESEARCH MAY WISH TO CONSULT THE REFERENCES AS A SPRINGBOARD TO YOUR OWN EVALUATION INTERESTS. SOME OF YOU MAY FIND THAT THIS SUMMARY MEETS YOUR NEEDS AND THAT YOU DO NOT HAVE TO CONSULT ANY OF THE REFERENCE MATERIALS CITED.

1. Students' perceptions were often inconsistent when their responses to individual items in the 32-item questionnaire were compared. For example, many students reported feeling motivated throughout the course and not intimidated by the technology. However, they also felt they were not in control of their learning needs and that they were less able to focus in the Video Learning environment than in a classroom setting. These group responses are perhaps more understandable when individual differences are considered. A more detailed analysis of individual responses revealed that the students who changed their learning strategies (that is, adapted to Video Learning) felt more in control than those who did not.
2. Approximately 80 percent of the students claimed that they participated less actively in the videoconference than they would in a classroom. A significant minority of these students attributed their lack of participation to poor sound quality. Otherwise, the students were quite satisfied with the other classroom arrangements, such as camera shots and lighting.
3. Although videoconferencing permits two-way interaction, the instructors did not use this feature for a number of reasons. Chugh's discovery that the students were dissatisfied with their ability to participate in the videoconference confirms how important it is to learners that instructors avoid the temptation to lecture.
4. Instructor responses to their 19-item questionnaire indicated highly individual perceptions of whether they could interact freely with the students, whether they could see non-verbal cues and a host of other issues. They were more diverse in their reactions than were the students.
5. The majority of instructors agreed, however, that they felt they were responsive to their students, considered videoconferencing more difficult and less relaxed than classroom teaching, had to change their teaching styles and found that videoconferencing offered less flexibility than the classroom environment. They also reported investing two to three times more effort in preparing for the videoconferencing course than for comparable time in the classroom.

While these reactions may seem to be less enthusiastic than those reported elsewhere, remember that in Chapter 4 Chugh recommended a number of steps that could be taken to address these problems. She also reported that the majority of both instructors and students would participate in another Video Learning course.

THIS EVALUATION IS TYPICAL OF OTHERS THAT DESCRIBE PROBLEMS THAT RELATE TO THE WAY VIDEO LEARNING IS ACTUALLY USED, NOT ITS INHERENT POTENTIAL. FOR EXAMPLE, IF PARTICIPANTS FEEL A LOSS OF CONTROL OVER THEIR LEARNING, THE PROBLEM MIGHT BE THAT THE INSTRUCTOR OVERUSES THE LECTURE FORMAT.

IMPLEMENTATION ISSUES Colin Latchem in Curtin, Australia, and Margaret Haughey in Edmonton, Canada, present a number of practical points arising from their research. From his review of the literature (1994), most of which

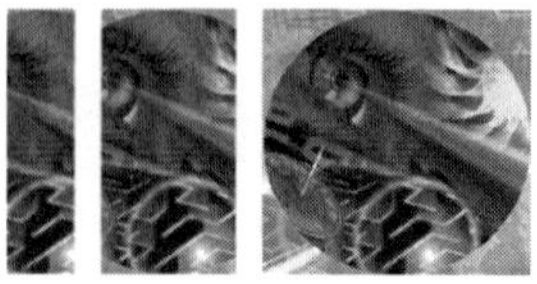

THE RECOMMENDED TECHNIQUES INCLUDE MANY OF THOSE DESCRIBED IN CHAPTER 7.

described Australian projects using videoconferencing, Colin indicates that Video Learning works particularly well when:

1. instructors have received appropriate training in using videoconferencing effectively, adopt a conversational style of presentation and prepare for and encourage voluntary contributions by all participants
2. students are given time to overcome any self-consciousness they may have about being on-camera
3. instructors direct their questions to specific students by name and give them time to consider their responses — time is particularly important if an open-ended question (e.g., what do you think?) has been asked
4. other media are integrated into the presentation and careful consideration is given to the design and legibility of the visuals
5. sessions are relatively short, involve a fairly small number of people and contain variety
6. the surroundings elicit feelings of comfort and security, and both room layout and technical configurations are designed to accommodate varied demands

Margaret Haughey (1993) reported on a number of instructional and organizational issues that arose from her evaluation of eight courses offered in a 1992-93 pilot series at the University of Alberta. Her evaluation techniques included observation, document review, questionnaires, group discussions and individual interviews. She concluded the following:

1. The appropriate use of the visual elements is critical.
2. A minimum disruption of the instructors' preferred teaching strategies is possible.
3. Most difficulties are of short-term duration.
4. Technical problems tend to be minimal but technical backup is essential.
5. Associated services such as fax, backup telephone access and photocopying are essential at each site.
6. The use of the design in which an instructor and students are at one site and other sites have "only" students requires further exploration of appropriate instructional strategies.
7. The students enjoyed meeting people from other sites in person if the occasion arose.
8. If facilities that serve a number of videoconferencing functions are used, the arrangement of the room should be adjusted as necessary so that it is appropriate to each type of videoconferencing application.
9. If it is an evening learning event, safe access to the building should be ensured.
10. Instructors preferred to teach from the institutional setting, not at a "borrowed" off-campus site.
11. The costs of partnership services, such as access to an underutilized room equipped with videoconferencing equipment, are likely to rise.

When we talked to Margaret as we prepared this book, she mentioned the need to evaluate the ethics of Video Learning behaviors. For example, what should participants do if people come into the room during a session, do not introduce themselves and remain off-camera? Do the participants have an obligation to tell the participants at the the other sites? In her view: "It is important that participants know who their listeners are. Visitors should be introduced (briefly). In many courses, personal anecdotes are used and could be a source of embarrassment. Trust and confidentiality are impossible without these protocols."

CONCLUSION

In this chapter you reviewed Kirkpatrick's four levels of evaluation and learned the extent to which they have been applied to Video Learning. You read some of the highlights of research done on teaching and learning issues and learned about some of the implementation issues that came up in other evaluations.

Our examination of the fundamentals of Video Learning is now complete. We look forward to hearing and reading about your experiences once you too become a user of Video Learning. There are many ways to be successful. Don't be afraid to experiment and find your own unique variation on the themes presented in this book and videotape.

References

Burge, E. J., & Roberts, J. M. (1998). *Classrooms with a difference: Facilitating learning on the Information Highway* (2nd ed.). Montréal, QC: Chenelière/McGraw-Hill.

Chugh, U. (1993). *Evaluation of a graduate videoconferencing course: Students' and instructors' perspective.* Calgary, AB: University of Calgary, Centre for Distance Learning and Innovative Technologies.

Haughey, M. (1993, October). *The University of Alberta and Alberta Transportation and Utilities Videoconferencing Project, 1992-93.* An evaluation report. Edmonton, AB: University of Alberta.

Kirkpatrick, D. L. (1996). *Evaluating training programs: The four levels.* San Francisco, CA: Berrett-Koehler.

Latchem, C. (1994). *Applications of compressed digital videoconferencing for the delivery of education, training and community services–national and international findings.* Australia: Curtin University of Technology.

Russell, T. L. (1992, October). Television's indelible impact on distance education: What we should have learned from comparative research. *Research in Distance Education,* pp. 2-4.

———. *The "No Significant Difference" phenomenon.* Unpublished paper. Raleigh, NC: North Carolina State University, Office of Instructional Telecommunications.

Transport Canada, Training Directorate. (1993, October). *Videoconferencing technology as a medium for distance learning.* Ottawa, ON: Author.

CONCLUSION

The major points and findings presented in this book and its companion videotape are emerging as the conventional wisdom about Video Learning. Here are the six that we think are the most important.

1. The challenge of facilitating Video Learning effectively is understanding how to adapt your instructional strengths and weaknesses to its characteristics.
2. Teaching and learning activities are varied and can present an opportunity, not a barrier, as you adapt your classroom techniques.
3. Planning and preparation are critical at every juncture, whether they involve conducting an appropriate needs assessment, preparing visual materials, "rehearsing" or using the equipment.
4. Seeking out colleagues who can assist you in a team-based approach is crucial to success. A learning designer should, we believe, be an integral part of the team and will have skills regarding Video Learning that complement your content knowledge and classroom teaching abilities.
5. To be an effective Video Learning instructor, pay attention to issues such as how visual materials should look, how to use your voice and how the technology works.
6. In designing your evaluation, include opportunities for learners to comment on the learning processes early and often, but be mindful of the opportunity to contribute to the field by evaluating outcomes and impact once the Video Learning sessions are completed.

We hope this book and the videotape have met your needs, and we wish you success in facilitating Video Learning. We look forward to hearing your stories should you wish to share them.

Appendix 1

EVALUATION FORMS

This Appendix contains three examples of evaluation forms used in the case studies described in Chapter 4: (1) the Bell/ARF VideoLink Project, (2) The University of Calgary Graduate Engineering Degree and (3) East Carolina University. They vary in length and complexity, illustrating the wide range of approaches currently being used.

ADDICTION RESEARCH FOUNDATION
Course Evaluation

This was the first time the Addiction Research Foundation has delivered an entire course using videoconferencing. To help us better plan future videoconference training events, please take a few minutes to complete the following questions.

Section A

1. Overall, how would you describe your experience of a course delivered by videoconference compared to a typical classroom course?

   ❑ better
   ❑ about the same
   ❑ worse

2. How would you describe the way you are able to interact with a presenter via videoconference compared to a typical classroom course?

   ❑ better
   ❑ about the same
   ❑ worse

3. To what extent did your group engage in discussion among yourselves during the presentation?

   ❑ a lot
   ❑ some
   ❑ not at all

4. How helpful was the group discussion mentioned in the last question in allowing you to meet your learning needs?

   ❑ very helpful
   ❑ helpful
   ❑ not very helpful
   ❑ not at all helpful

Please comment:

____

____

____

____

---

5. How important was it for you to see a close-up shot of the person who was speaking?

   - ❑ very important
   - ❑ important
   - ❑ somewhat important
   - ❑ not at all important

6. To what extent is it helpful to participate in training events that are offered for a few hours a week over several weeks rather than events offered over several consecutive days of training?

   - ❑ very helpful
   - ❑ helpful
   - ❑ somewhat helpful
   - ❑ not at all helpful

Please comment:

____
____
____
____
____

7. Would you be willing to pay higher registration fees for a course delivered by videoconference compared to a classroom course offered in Toronto if you saved money related to travel?

   - ❑ yes
   - ❑ no

8. Overall, how would you rate the sound quality during the videoconference?

   - ❑ excellent
   - ❑ good
   - ❑ fair
   - ❑ poor

9. Overall, how would you describe the picture quality during the videoconference?

- ❑ excellent
- ❑ good
- ❑ fair
- ❑ poor

10. Overall, how would you rate the quality of the overheads displayed on the television monitors during the videoconference?

- ❑ excellent
- ❑ good
- ❑ fair
- ❑ poor

11. For each of the statements below, please indicate the extent to which each is a concern for you in deciding whether to attend future training events delivered by videoconference. Please circle the number that best describes your feelings. Please do not mark in between a number.

a. Lack of "in-person" contact with instructors.

very much a concern 1--------2--------3--------4 **not at all a concern**

b. Lack of "in-person" contact with course participants in other sites.

very much a concern 1--------2--------3--------4 **not at all a concern**

c. Convenient access to a videoconference facility.

very much a concern 1--------2--------3--------4 **not at all a concern**

d. Technical quality of the sound.

very much a concern 1--------2--------3--------4 **not at all a concern**

e. Technical quality of the video.

very much 1--------2--------3--------4 **not at all**
a concern **a concern**

f. Fewer chances to travel to large centers for training courses and workshops.

very much 1--------2--------3--------4 **not at all**
a concern **a concern**

g. Higher registration fees for events delivered by videoconferencing.

very much 1--------2--------3--------4 **not at all**
a concern **a concern**

Please note any other concerns you may have about videoconferencing, not mentioned in the list above:

____

12. What did you like most about the videoconference experience?

____

13. What did you like least about the videoconference experience?

____

14. How willing would you be to participate in another training event delivered by videoconferencing?

- ❑ very willing
- ❑ willing
- ❑ somewhat willing
- ❑ not at all willing

15. Overall, how satisfied were you with the videoconference experience?

- ❑ very satisfied
- ❑ satisfied
- ❑ somewhat satisfied
- ❑ not at all satisfied

16. Have you ever participated in an "audio only" teleconference?

- ❑ yes
- ❑ no

17. How many training events did you attend in the previous 12 months?

Please indicate number of training events:_______

18. What is the average length of the training events you attend?

- ❑ half-day
- ❑ 1 to 2 days
- ❑ 3 to 4 days
- ❑ 5 days or more

19. On average, what proportion of training events would you attend in an average year that require overnight travel?

- ❑ over 75 %
- ❑ between 50 % and 75 %
- ❑ between 25 % and 50 %
- ❑ less than 25 %

20. To what extent did the course you have just taken meet your needs?

- ❑ very well
- ❑ well
- ❑ somewhat well
- ❑ not at all well

Please comment:

21. How effectively was the course material delivered?

- ❑ very effectively
- ❑ effectively
- ❑ somewhat effectively
- ❑ not at all effectively

Please comment:

How would you describe the level of interaction between the participants and the instructors?

- ❑ excellent
- ❑ good
- ❑ fair
- ❑ poor

Please comment:

Overall, how satisfied were you with the course?

- ❑ very satisfied
- ❑ satisfied
- ❑ somewhat satisfied
- ❑ not at all satisfied

Please comment:

____

____

____

____

____

ENCI 619.96

Use of Videoconferencing for Course Delivery

Student's Perspective

For the following statements please circle the number that best fits your situation or opinion on a 5 point scale of agreement or scale of effectiveness, as the case may be.

A. **Student's Learning Style**

1. I felt motivated to learn during the entire course.

   Strongly Disagree_____________________________Strongly Agree
   1 2 3 4 5

2. All throughout this course I felt I was in control of my learning needs.

   Strongly Disagree_____________________________Strongly Agree
   1 2 3 4 5

   Comments: ____
   ____

3. I was intimidated by the videoconferencing technology used to deliver this course.

   Strongly Disagree_____________________________Strongly Agree
   1 2 3 4 5

   Comments: ____
   ____

4. My comfort level with the technology improved as the course progressed.

   Strongly Disagree_____________________________Strongly Agree
   1 2 3 4 5

5. I am usually more focussed in the face-to-face classroom than I was during this course.

   Strongly Disagree_____________________________Strongly Agree
   1 2 3 4 5

6. I followed the course content more closely when the instructor was at the local site compared to when he was at the remote site.

Strongly Disagree______________________________Strongly Agree
1 2 3 4 5

Comments: ____

____

7. I usually participate more in face-to-face classes than I did in this videoconferencing course.

Strongly Disagree______________________________Strongly Agree
1 2 3 4 5

Comments: ____

____

8. The technology influenced my lack of participation in this course.

Strongly Disagree______________________________Strongly Agree
1 2 3 4 5

9. Interaction with the students at the local site helped me to understand the material.

Strongly Disagree______________________________Strongly Agree
1 2 3 4 5

10. The classroom facilities were adequate.

Strongly Disagree______________________________Strongly Agree
1 2 3 4 5

11. I learned as well by videoconferencing as I usually do in a face-to-face class.

Strongly Disagree______________________________Strongly Agree
1 2 3 4 5

B. Course Content

12. The amount of material covered was too much for the length of this course.

Strongly Disagree______________________________Strongly Agree
1 2 3 4 5

13. There was agreement between announced course objectives and what was taught.

Strongly Disagree______________________________Strongly Agree
1 2 3 4 5

14. This course improved my understanding of concepts and principles in this field.

Strongly Disagree______________________________Strongly Agree
1 2 3 4 5

15. The course was taught as effectively as traditional face-to-face instruction.

Strongly Disagree______________________________Strongly Agree
1 2 3 4 5

C. **Instructors**

16. Overall the instructor was responsive to the learning needs of the students.

Strongly Disagree______________________________Strongly Agree
1 2 3 4 5

17. In responding to a query from the students at the remote site, overall the reaction time from the instructors was about the same as in face-to-face instruction.

Strongly Disagree______________________________Strongly Agree
1 2 3 4 5

Comments: ____

____

18. When the session was delivered from the remote site, rather than local, I was very aware of the fact the instructor was not present in person.

Strongly Disagree______________________________Strongly Agree
1 2 3 4 5

Comments: ____

____

19. There was immediate feedback concerning issues of content and assignments from the instructors teaching at the other site.

Strongly Disagree______________________________Strongly Agree
1 2 3 4 5

Comments: ____
____

20. The instructor(s) provided sufficient opportunity for interaction.

Strongly Disagree______________________________Strongly Agree
1 2 3 4 5

Comments: ____
____

D. Course Package

21. The course material was easy to follow.

Strongly Disagree______________________________Strongly Agree
1 2 3 4 5

22. The course material was relevant and effective in assisting me with my learning.

Strongly Disagree______________________________Strongly Agree
1 2 3 4 5

23. The cost of the course material was reasonable.

Strongly Disagree______________________________Strongly Agree
1 2 3 4 5

E. Technology

24. The technology provided ample opportunity to discuss concerns related to assignments.

Strongly Disagree______________________________Strongly Agree
1 2 3 4 5

25. Taking this course, through videoconferencing, has changed my learning strategies or approaches.

Strongly Disagree____________________________Strongly Agree
1 2 3 4 5

Comments: ____
____

26. The technology used to deliver this course was effective and did not pose any barrier to "visual interactions" i.e. facial expression and body language.

Strongly Disagree____________________________Strongly Agree
1 2 3 4 5

27. The whiteboard used to write on was effective in presenting the course material.

Strongly Disagree____________________________Strongly Agree
1 2 3 4 5

28. Size and clarity of the camera shots were satisfactory.

Strongly Disagree____________________________Strongly Agree
1 2 3 4 5

29. The audio-visual procedures were logically integrated and effectively presented.

Strongly Disagree____________________________Strongly Agree
1 2 3 4 5

30. The quality of sound was satisfactory throughout the length of the course.

Strongly Disagree____________________________Strongly Agree
1 2 3 4 5

31. The lighting of the local site was adequate.

Strongly Disagree____________________________Strongly Agree
1 2 3 4 5

32. I interacted with the students at the local site more frequently compared with the students at the other site.

Strongly Disagree____________________________Strongly Agree
1 2 3 4 5

G. Socio-Demographics

1. Gender: _____ male _____ female

2. Age: _____ under 25 _____ 26-35
_____ 36-45 _____ over 46

3. Are you currently enrolled in a degree program? ___ yes ___ no

If yes, which degree program? ______________________________

4. Have you attended distance delivered courses prior to this one?
___ yes ___ no

If yes, were they (check all that apply):
_____ correspondence _____ video teleconferencing
_____ audio teleconferencing _____ other, please specify ______

5. Why did you choose this method of study?
_____ a) course was not available in a face-to-face format
_____ b) time and location were more convenient than travelling to campus
_____ c) I was interested in the delivery technology
_____ d) other, please specify______________________________

6. Would you take another course delivered by videoconferencing?
___ yes ___ no

Thank you for your participation and time in completing this questionnaire.

Source: Irena Kirek & Urmil Chugh. ***Use of Videoconferencing for Course Delivery.***

ENCI 619.96

Use of Videoconferencing for Graduate Course for Engineers

Instructor's Perspective

A. The following statements are concerned with videoconferencing as a medium of instruction/learning. Please indicate your opinion by circling the appropriate number on the agreement scale.

1. Videoconferencing is an effective medium for teaching.

   Strongly Disagree________________________Strongly Agree
   1 2 3 4 5

   Comments: ____
   ____

2. This course was taught as effectively (or better) compared with the traditional face-to-face method.

   Strongly Disagree________________________Strongly Agree
   1 2 3 4 5

   Comments: ____
   ____

3. During this course I was as responsive to the needs of the students as I am in the traditional face-to-face classroom.

   Strongly Disagree________________________Strongly Agree
   1 2 3 4 5

   Comments: ____
   ____

4. I was frustrated when I could not see all the students at the remote site on the local screen.

   Strongly Disagree________________________Strongly Agree
   1 2 3 4 5

   Comments: ____
   ____

5. I focused more on the students at the remote site compared with the students at the local site.

Strongly Disagree_______________________________Strongly Agree
1 2 3 4 5

Comments: ____
____

6. I was aware of the fact that the students at the remote site were not present in person.

Strongly Disagree_______________________________Strongly Agree
1 2 3 4 5

Comments: ____
____

7. Size and clarity of the camera shots were not satisfactory.

Strongly Disagree_______________________________Strongly Agree
1 2 3 4 5

Comments: ____
____

8. The quality of sound was satisfactory throughout the length of the course.

Strongly Disagree_______________________________Strongly Agree
1 2 3 4 5

Comments: ____
____

9. I interacted with the students as much as I would in the face-to-face classroom.

Strongly Disagree_______________________________Strongly Agree
1 2 3 4 5

Comments: ____
____

10. I spent about the same time preparing for this course as I would for the face-to-face instruction.

Strongly Disagree_____________________________Strongly Agree
1 2 3 4 5

Comments: ____
____

B. Demographics

1. You are a faculty member at:
____ The University of Calgary ______ University of Alberta

2. Have you taught graduate distance education courses prior to teaching this course?
___ yes ___ no

If yes, it was (or they were)
____ Correspondence ____ Audio teleconferencing
____ Video teleconferencing ____ Other

C. In closing, can you please answer the following questions:

1. In future, would you consider conducting more graduate courses through video-conferencing?
____ Yes _____ No ______ Undecided

2. Can you briefly comment on likes, dislikes and problems you encountered during the length of the course.

____

____

____

____

____

3. It has been said and I quote: "In the face-to-face classroom, the students are on your turf, you are in control (mostly). When things go wrong you can quietly excuse yourself and go outside to collect your wits. The video classroom does not leave that kind of room for manoeuvres. Students control their end of the interaction. That becomes really obvious when you discover they can switch off the microphones and chat amongst themselves."

   What are your thoughts on this matter?

   ____

   ____

   ____

   ____

   ____

Source: Irena Kirek & Urmil Chugh. *Use of Videoconferencing for Course Delivery.*

S • A • M • P • L • E

EAST CAROLINA UNIVERSITY

SUPPLEMENTAL STUDENT REACTION SHEET FOR INTERACTIVE TELEVISION COURSES

COURSE NUMBER ______________________ SEMESTER__________________

INSTRUCTOR____

Please circle one response per item based on the following scale:

SD	D	U/NA	A	SA
Strongly disagree	Disagree	Undecided or not applicable	Agree	Strongly agree

TECHNICAL QUALITY

1. In general, I could see the instructor clearly.	SD	D	U/NA	A	SA
2. In general, I could hear the instructor clearly.	SD	D	U/NA	A	SA
3. In general, I could see the students at the remote sites clearly.	SD	D	U/NA	A	SA
4. In general, I could hear the students at the remote sites clearly.	SD	D	U/NA	A	SA
5. In general, I could see the "slides" or graphics clearly.	SD	D	U/NA	A	SA
6. In general, very little disturbing background noise was transmitted through the system.	SD	D	U/NA	A	SA

COMMENTS____

____

ENVIRONMENT

7. The room temperature was usually comfortable.	SD	D	U/NA	A	SA
8. The room lighting was adequate.	SD	D	U/NA	A	SA
9. In general, there was very little noise or distraction from outside the room.	SD	D	U/NA	A	SA
10. The room arrangement was optimal.	SD	D	U/NA	A	SA

S • A • M • P • L • E

EAST CAROLINA UNIVERSITY

COMMENTS____

____

COURSE DYNAMICS/DESIGN

11. I had enough opportunities to ask questions of the instructor IN CLASS.	SD	D	U/NA	A	SA
12. I had enough opportunities to ask questions of the instructor OUTSIDE OF CLASS.	SD	D	U/NA	A	SA
13. I had enough opportunities to talk with other students IN MY CLASS.	SD	D	U/NA	A	SA
14. The instructor successfully engaged students at ALL SITES in dialog.	SD	D	U/NA	A	SA
15. In general, the display of graphics was well-coordinated with the lecture/discussion.	SD	D	U/NA	A	SA
16. In general, I was able to follow along when the instructor referred to off-screen material, such as handouts, diagrams and textbooks.	SD	D	U/NA	A	SA
17. In general, the instructor looked into the proper camera when addressing students at remote sites.	SD	D	U/NA	A	SA
18. In general, the instructor adapted well if/when technical difficulties arose.	SD	D	U/NA	A	SA

COMMENTS____

____

RESOURCES

19. I had adequate access to LIBRARY resources (including CD-ROM) for my papers and projects.	SD	D	U/NA	A	SA
20. The use of LIBRARY resources increased my understanding of the course content.	SD	D	U/NA	A	SA
21. I had adequate access to ELECTRONIC MAIL for communication with my instructor and/or other students.	SD	D	U/NA	A	SA

S • A • M • P • L • E

EAST CAROLINA UNIVERSITY

22. The use of ELECTRONIC MAIL increased my understanding of the course content.	SD	D	U/NA	A	SA
23. I had adequate access to INTERNET resources (such as Listservs, Gophers, World Wide Web) for my papers and projects.	SD	D	U/NA	A	SA
24. The use of INTERNET resources increased my understanding of the course content.	SD	D	U/NA	A	SA
25. The site facilitator was helpful in dealing with technical and other problems.	SD	D	U/NA	A	SA

COMMENTS____

____

GENERAL

26. The video office hours were helpful.	SD	D	U/NA	A	SA
27. The telephone office hours were helpful.	SD	D	U/NA	A	SA
28. This course met my expectations.	SD	D	U/NA	A	SA
29. I would recommend this course to others.	SD	D	U/NA	A	SA

30. The information I learned from this course will be or has been helpful in my job.

    PLEASE EXPLAIN.____

____

31. Did the course make you think? Did it give you any new insights?

    PLEASE EXPLAIN.____

____

32. Would you take another course via **distance learning?** WHY OR WHY NOT?

____

____

33. Would you have been able to take this course if it **hadn't** been offered at a distance?

    _____ yes _____ no PLEASE EXPLAIN.____

____

S • A • M • P • L • E

EAST CAROLINA UNIVERSITY

34. What did you like the **most** about this course?______________________________

____

35. Is there any way this course can be improved? If so, please list suggestions.

____

____

36. Please note the effectiveness of the following methods or media used during class on this scale:

1	2	3	4	5
Not effective	Somewhat effective	Effective	Very effective	Not applicable (didn't see)

___ lecture
___ class discussion
___ graphics (slides)
___ videotapes
___ CD-ROM program
___ course-mate
___ handouts
___ textbook
___ group activities

37. How did you hear of this course? (check all that apply)

___ my advisor
___ ECU off-campus graduate course listing
___ flyer/brochure
___ local newspaper
___ colleague
___ others: specify ______________________________

38. OTHER COMMENTS?____

____

THANKS VERY MUCH! YOUR FEEDBACK WILL HELP US IMPROVE THIS AND FUTURE DISTANCE LEARNING COURSES!

Source: East Carolina University, Greenville, North Carolina, U.S.A.

Appendix 2

SAMPLE VISUAL MATERIALS

Sandra Hodder, from the Ontario Learning and Technology Exchange Consortium (OLTEC), shares these examples of visual materials designed one way for presentation in the print format and two other ways for presentation during Video Learning sessions using an overhead projector and a document camera.

DOCUMENT 1
for Overhead Projector

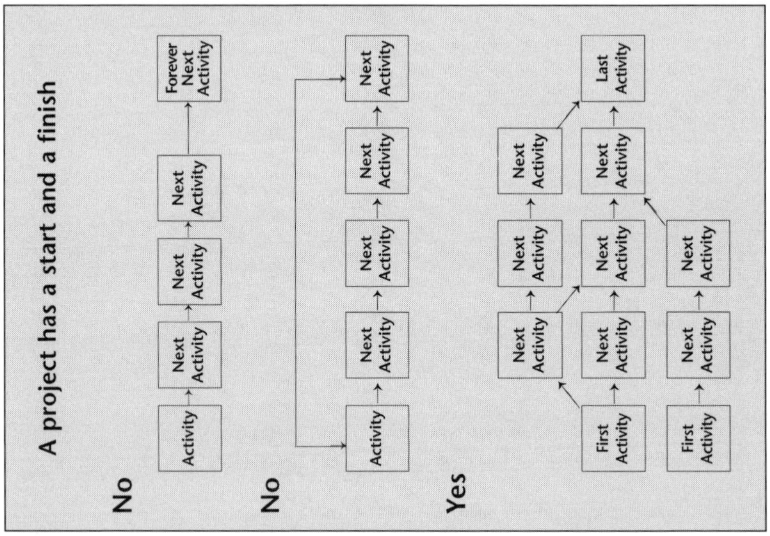

DOCUMENT 2
for Document Camera

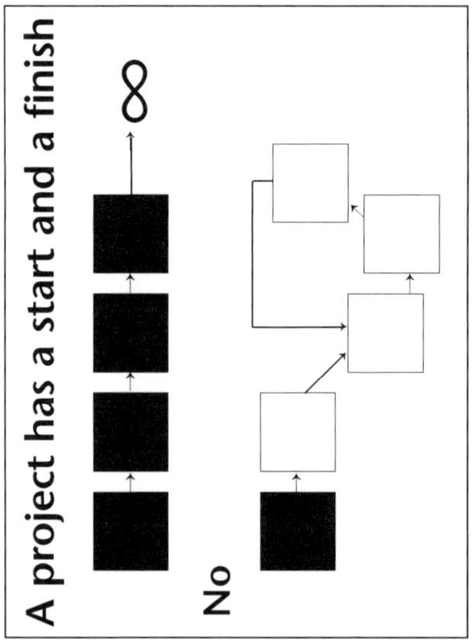

DOCUMENT 3
for Print Handout

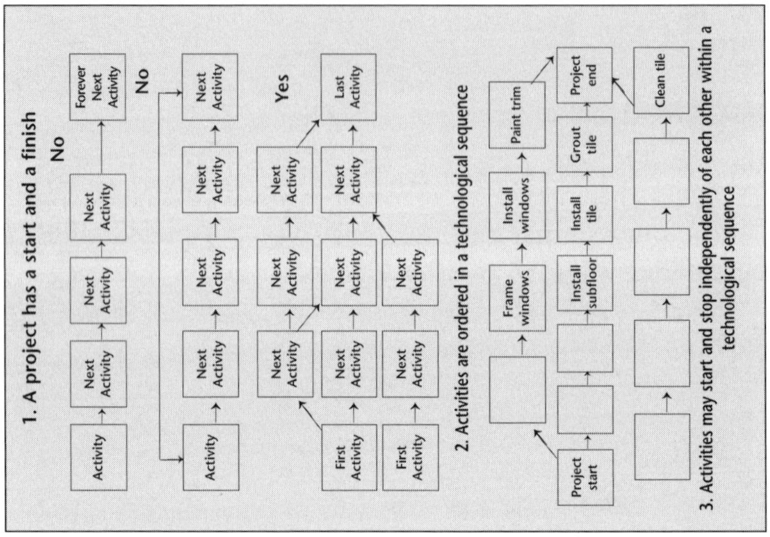

	DOCUMENT 1 for Overhead Projector	DOCUMENT 2 for Document Camera	DOCUMENT 3 for Print Handout
Method of display	Overhead projector	Document camera — either slide show or paper or overhead	Print — handout for participants
Orientation	Portrait — progressive disclosure of segments would be used.	Landscape — all the content is seen at one time.	Portrait — all the content is seen at one time.
Font size	Can be 12 or 14 points as the projector increases the image.	Must be much larger — 24 to 30 points.	Is much smaller — normal print fonts 10 to 12 points.
Number of needed visuals to contain the content	One	Two needed to permit the font size increases and diagram shape size increases.	One print page contains the material from 2 overheads or 3 document camera pages [slides]. Here the objective is to save material production costs by using less paper.
Words and labels	Normal labeling guidelines would be used.	Small words are removed altogether. Color is used more effectively to contain content and direct the eye.	Small words for labels are present. Here the purpose is to provide as much detail as necessary so the learner has accurate notes.
Use of symbols and pictures	It is always a good idea to find a symbol to replace a phrase as it is a memory aid.	Using symbols and pictures is even more important here as one would strive for less complexity. Note how the infinity symbol has replaced the words «Forever Next Activity.»	Here, the highest level of detail can be used. Pictures and symbols make the handout more interesting for the learner and more inviting to use afterwards to review the content.

Source: Sandra Hodder, Sheridan College, Oakville, Ontario.

Further Readings

Chapter 1
When and Why Should I Use Video Learning?

Aubé, S., Chilibeck, M., & Wright, D. (1996). *Cost analysis of video conferencing for distance education at the University of Ottawa.* Working Paper 96-45. Presented at First Annual Meeting & Conference, TeleLearning-NCE. Constructing a vision for the Knowledge Society. November 5-7, Sheraton Centre Hotel, Montréal, Québec.

Bates, A. W. (1995). *Technology, open learning and distance education.* London, UK: Routledge.

———. (1991). *Technology in open learning and distance education: A guide for decision-makers.* Booklet Three: Selecting technologies. Vancouver, BC: The Commonwealth of Learning/Open Learning Agency.

Burge, E. J., & Roberts, J. M. (1998). *Classrooms with a Difference: Facilitating learning on the Information Highway* (2nd ed.). Montréal, QC: Chenelière/McGraw-Hill.

Cukier, J. (1996). *Cost-benefit analysis of telelearning: Developing a methodology framework.* Presented at First Annual Meeting & Conference, TeleLearning-NCE. Constructing a vision for the Knowledge Society. November 5-7, Sheraton Centre Hotel, Montréal, Québec.

Dhanarajan, G., Ip, P. K., Yuen, K. S., & Swales, C. (Eds.). (1994). *Economics of distance education: Recent experience.* Hong Kong: Open Learning Institute Press.

Haughey, M., & Anderson, T. (1998). *Networked learning: The pedagogy of the Internet.* Montréal, QC: Chenelière/McGraw-Hill.

Havelock, R. G. with Zlotolow, S. (1994). *The change agent's guide* (2nd ed.). Englewood Cliffs, NJ: Educational Technology Publishers.

MacDonald, D. (1998). *Audio and audiographic learning: The cornerstone of the Information Highway.* Montréal, QC: Chenelière/McGraw-Hill.

Rogers, E. (1983). *Diffusion of innovations* (3rd ed.). New York, NY: Free Press.

Rogers, E. M., & Shoemaker, F. F. (1971). *Communication of innovations: A cross-cultural approach.* New York, NY: Free Press.

Chapter 2
How Does Video Learning Equipment Work?

Boomstein, D. (1994). Desktop conferencing. In P. S. Portway & C. Lane (Eds.), *Guide to teleconferencing and distance learning,* (2nd ed., pp. 79-87). Livermore, CA: Applied Business teleCommunications.

Brooksby, R. (1994). Two-way interactive video. In P. S. Portway & C. Lane (Eds.), *Guide to teleconferencing and distance learning* (2nd ed., pp. 57-68). Livermore, CA: Applied Business teleCommunications.

Cass, E. (Ed.). (1992). *Video-conferencing in open and distance learning: A guide to current developments.* Burnaby, BC: The Open Learning Agency.

Giles, S. (1997). Desktop videoconferencing support for remote training. In *The new learning environment: A global perspective* (p. 241). Conference Abstracts, The 18th ICDE World Conference, June 2-6. University Park: PennState.

Knowledge Connection Corporation. (1995). *Technology and learning: Innovative projects in Ontario in 1995.* Prepared by N. McKinnon, A. Stahmer, & L. Green. Toronto, ON: Author.

———. (1996). *Technology and learning: Innovative projects 1996.* Prepared by N. McKinnon, A. Stahmer, & L. Green. Toronto, ON: Author.

Portway, P. S. (1994). Desktop. In P. S. Portway & C. Lane (Eds.), *Guide to teleconferencing and distance learning* (2nd ed., pp. 69-87). Livermore, CA: Applied Business teleCommunications.

Webster, J. (In press). Desktop videoconferencing: Still wary after all these years? Paper submitted to Special Issue on Intensive Research in Information Systems: Using Qualitative, Interpretive and Case Methods to Study Information Technology. MIS Quarterly.

Chapter 3
What Resources Will I Need?

Bates, A. W. (1995). *Technology, open learning and distance education.* London, UK: Routledge.

Kirkwood, B. (n.d.) *Distance education using electronic means: A "Rapid Prototype."* Unpublished report. Toronto, ON: Purchasing Management Association of Canada.

Pacey, L. M., & Penney, W. P. (1995). Thinking strategically: Reshaping the face of distance education and open learning. In J. M. Roberts & E. M. Keough (Eds.), *Why the Information Highway? Lessons from open and distance learning* (pp. 13-39). Toronto, ON: Trifolium Books Inc.

Roberts, J. M., & Keough, E. M. (Eds.). (1995). *Why the Information Highway? Lessons from open and distance learning.* Toronto, ON: Trifolium Books Inc.

Chapter 4
How Can I Learn from Other People's Experiences?

Forsgren & Associates. (1993). *Meetings at a distance: A practical guide for videoconferencing meeting leaders.* Saint John, NB: Author.

Hakes, B., Couchenour, J., Rezabek, L., & Sachs, S. (1995). *Compressed video for instruction: Operations and applications.* Revised and enlarged. Washington, DC: The Association for Educational Communications and Technology.

Hakes, B. T., Sachs, S. G., Box, J., & Couchenour, J. (1993). *Compressed video: Operations and applications.* Washington, DC: The Association for Educational Communications and Technology.

Hebert, W. S. (1997). *Access through innovation: Videoconferencing using satellite and terrestrial technology to deliver education and training at a distance.* Thunder Bay, ON: Contact North/Contact Nord.

Hunt, J. L., & Ballantyne, G. W. (1993, January). The Guelph-Waterloo video link. *Physics in Canada/La Physique au Canada,* 57-59.

Knowledge Connection Corporation. (1995). *Technology and learning: Innovative projects in Ontario in 1995.* Prepared by N. McKinnon, A. Stahmer, & L. Green. Toronto, ON: Author.

———. (1996). *Technology and learning: Innovative projects 1996.* Prepared by N. McKinnon, A. Stahmer, & L. Green. Toronto, ON: Author.

McDonell, D. J. (1995). Audio, audio graphics, compressed video, computer conferencing and the Internet: Distance education at the University of Ottawa. In H. Maurer (Ed.), *Proceedings of ED-MEDIA 95 World Conference on Educational Multimedia and Hypermedia* (pp. 454-459). Charlottesville, VA: Association for the Advancement of Computing in Education.

Moore, M. G., & Koble, M. A. (Eds.). (1995). *Video-based telecommunications in distance education.* Number 4 in the series *Readings in Distance Education.* University Park, PA: The Pennsylvania State University, American Center for the Study of Distance Education.

Shale, D., & Kirek, I. (1997). Interactive videoconferencing: The next best thing to being there? In *The new learning environment:* A global perspective (p. 109). Conference Abstracts, The 18th ICDE World Conference, June 2-6. University Park, PA: PennState.

Smyth, E., & Tobin, L. (1997). *Using videoconferencing as a mode of curriculum delivery for learners with special needs in small communities.* Sudbury, ON: Contact North/Contact Nord.

Chapter 5
What Active Learning Principles Should I Use?

Brindley, J. (1995). Learners and learner services: The key to the future. In J. M. Roberts & E. M. Keough (Eds.), *Why the Information Highway? Lessons from open and distance learning* (pp. 102-125). Toronto, ON: Trifolium Books Inc.

Burge, E. J. (1995). Electronic highway or weaving loom? Thinking about conferencing technologies for learning. In F. Lockwod (Ed.), *Open and distance learning today* (pp. 151-163). London, UK: Routledge.

Lamy, T. (1995). *Videocommunication: A faculty guide to learning and communicating by compressed videoconferencing.* (J. Roberts, Trans.) Sudbury, ON: Laurentian University, Centre for Continuing Education. Aussi disponible en français.

MacKinnon, A., Walshe, B., Cummings, M., & Velonis, U. (1995). An inventory of pedagogical considerations for interactive television. *Journal of Distance Education/Revue de l'éducation à distance, X* (1), 75-94.

Mills, R., & Tait, R. (Eds.). (1996). *Supporting the learner in open and distance learning.* London, UK: Pitman Publishing.

Roberts, J., Brindley, J. E., & Spronk, B. (1998). *Learning on the Information Highway: A Learner's Guide.* Montréal, QC: Chenelière/McGraw-Hill.

Chapter 6
How Do I Prepare for Video Learning?

Dooley, L. M. (1997). Instructional use of compressed video teleconferencing: A report from faculty users. *ED Journal, 11*(2), J-11 to J-14.

Hakes, B., Couchenour, J., Rezabek, L., & Sachs, S. (1995). *Compressed video for instruction: Operations and applications.* Revised and enlarged. Washington, DC: The Association for Educational Communications and Technology.

Horton, W. (1995). *Illustrating computer documentation: The art of presenting information graphically and online.* New York, NY: Wiley.

Latchem, C., Mitchell, J., & Atkinson, R. (1993). Videoconferencing networks and applications in Australian Higher Education. In G. Davies & B. Samways, (Eds.), *Teleteaching. Proceedings of the International Federation for Information Processing,* Third Teleteaching Conference, Trondheim, Norway.

Office of Instructional Development. (1995). *Interactive video network: Faculty guide and technical training manual.* College Park: University of Maryland University College.

Chapter 7
How Do I Facilitate Video Learning?

Biner, P. M., Welch, K. D., Barone, N. M., Summers, M., & Dean, R. S. (1997). The impact of remote-site group size on student satisfaction and relative performance in interactive telecourses. *The American Journal of Distance Education, 11*(1), 23-33.

Bruce, M. A., & Shade, R. A. (1995, September). Effective teaching and learning strategies using compressed video. *Techtrends, 40*(4), 18-22.

Griffin, G. (1995). *Teaching tips: Teaching with compressed videoconferencing.* Waterloo, ON: University of Waterloo, Teaching Resources and Continuing Education (TRACE).

Haughey, M., & Jacobson, B. (1996). *Instructional strategies for multi-site videoconferencing.* Presented to the 12th Annual Canadian Association for Distance Education Conference, Université de Moncton, New Brunswick. May 22-25.

———. (1996, April). *Flipping the channels: Multiple-site videoconferencing.* Presented to the Standing Committee on Educational Technology (SCOET) Conference Connections 96, Vancouver, British Columbia.

Lawrence, B. H. (1995). Teaching and learning via videoconference: The benefits of cooperative learning. *Journal of Educational Technology Systems, 24*(2) 145-149.

Such, P. (n.d.). *Large class videoconferencing.* Unpublished paper. Toronto, ON: York University, Atkinson College. Paper available on request from author.

Chapter 8
How Do I Evaluate Video Learning?

Black, D., & Harasim, L. (1992, December). *The ISDN distance learning trial: Evaluation of Phase 1.* Burnaby, BC: Open Learning Agency.

Hackley, P., & Webster, J. (n.d.). *Initial recommendations for courses taught through the compressed-video distance telelearning facility.* Unpublished paper. Waterloo, ON: University of Waterloo.

Knott, T. (1994). *Planning & evaluating distance education: A guide to collaboration.* Memphis, TN: Diaphera Publications, publishers for American Academy of Distance Learning and Training.

Niemi, J. A., & Owens, K. (1996). Evaluation research for the development of effective practice in the video-teleconferencing distance education human resource development classroom. In E. F. Holton III (Ed.), *1996 Conference Proceedings.* Austin, TX: Academy of Human Resource Development.

Open Learning Technology Corporation Ltd. (1996). *Models for evaluating interactive video and videoconferencing.* http://www.oltc.edu.au/reports/models/modelsft.htm

Savenye, W., & Box, C. (1993). Evaluation techniques. In B. T. Hakes, S. G. Sachs, C. Box, & J. Couchenour (Eds.), *Compressed video: Operations and applications* (pp. 191-212). Washington, DC: The Association for Educational Communications and Technology.

Webster, J., & Hackley, P. (In press). Teaching effectiveness in technology-mediated distance learning. *Academy of Management Journal, 40*(6).

Glossary

ACTION RESEARCH A systematic and context-adaptive method of collecting and analyzing data to develop real-world, practical knowledge that could later lead to change in that context.

AFFECTIVE DOMAIN (see also COGNITIVE DOMAIN and PSYCHOMOTOR DOMAIN) One of three domains that form a hierarchy or taxonomy of educational objectives. This domain refers to the development of values, emotions and attitudes, and to the outlooks and behaviors that characterize each level of development.

ANALOG An electronic, non-digital signal that is in a continuous format, as opposed to a digital signal, which is discrete.

ASPECT RATIO The ratio of height to width in a visual image presented on paper or on a video or computer screen.

ASSOCIATION OF CANADIAN COMMUNITY COLLEGES (ACCC) A national organization of college-level educational institutions from provinces and territories across Canada.

ASYNCHRONOUS (see also DELAYED-TIME) Communication that occurs when learners and instructors are not linked at the same time. The originators of messages create and send the messages at a time convenient to them; the messages are stored until the recipients find it convenient to retrieve them. Letters, voice-mail messages and e-mail are all examples of asynchronous communication.

AUDIOCONFERENCING A technical arrangement in which three or more telephones or speakerphones are connected by a central device called a bridge so that people in three or more places can talk to one another.

AUDIOGRAPHIC CONFERENCING A technical arrangement in which audioconferencing (telephones or speakerphones and a bridge) is supplemented by graphic devices that send text or still pictures.

AUDIOGRAPHIC LEARNING (AGL) Learning that occurs when learners and instructors use telephone and graphics technologies (audiographic conferencing) to facilitate dialogue, exchange messages and access experts as part of a learning process.

AUDIOGRAPHICS TECHNOLOGIES (see also GROUPWARE) Devices that work on analog or digital telephone lines and facilitate the real-time exchange of text and still, color graphics information. Historically, such devices have been separate pieces of equipment.

AUDIO LEARNING (AL) Learning that occurs when learners and instructors use audioconferencing technology to engage in discussions, exchange messages and access experts as part of a formal or informal learning endeavor. All such interactions occur in real-time; the learners and instructors are present at different sites at the same time and must coordinate their schedules.

BACK-UP Create a duplicate copy.

BRIDGE A telecommunications device that links three or more telephone, computer or video terminals so that all participants can communicate.

BROWSER (see also SEARCH ENGINE) A software program that enables users to access and navigate the Internet and the WWW to find the content they want.

BULLETIN BOARD SYSTEM (BBS) A small computer system that allows members to exchange messages, maintain discussion groups and download software.

CAMERA SCAN AREA The area framed by the television camera. Since detail at the edge of the scanning area is sometimes lost, it is advisable to design information to fit within the safe area (the area within the border that is 10 percent smaller than the scanning area).

CHAT LINES Also called chat groups, chat lines are created using software programs that allow several users to interact through text-based conversations in real-time.

CLIENT Client in computer-network terminology can have two meanings. Sometimes it is synonymous with user. Other times it denotes a relationship between two computers, in which one is a host that serves a client machine. In the latter case, the client computer becomes a guest on the host computer in order to use the host computer's resources.

CODEC (ENCODER AND DECODER) An electronic device that converts analog signals to digital ones, usually incorporating a compression protocol. The codec encodes, or compresses, the signal at the transmitting end and decodes, or decompresses it, at the receiving end.

COGNITIVE DOMAIN (see also AFFECTIVE DOMAIN and PSYCHOMOTOR DOMAIN) The second of three domains that form a hierarchy or taxonomy of educational objectives, this domain is the most widely used. It refers to knowledge outcomes and the thinking skills that characterize each category of outcome. The higher the level of required outcome, the more sophisticated the thinking skills. Each category includes behaviors needed in prior categories.

COLLABORATIVE LEARNING A proactive approach to learning in which the learner interacts with peers to hear new information, compare different and sometimes conflicting points of view and life experiences and work cooperatively on instructor-directed or self-directed learning projects.

COMPACT DISC-READ ONLY MEMORY (CD-ROM) A disc that can store a large amount of text, audio, video and graphics information. Your computer needs a special device so these materials can be displayed on your screen, and it must meet certain minimal technical specifications for the device to work.

COMPRESSED VIDEO LEARNING (CVL) Learning that occurs when instructors and learners use microphones, cameras and other videoconferencing equipment to exchange verbal and moving color images to engage in discussions, exchange messages and talk to experts as part of a formal or informal learning process. All such interactions occur in real-time; that is, the learners and instructors are present at different sites at the same time and they must coordinate their schedules to do this.

COMPUSERVE One of many commercial Internet Service Providers.

COMPUTER CONFERENCING A central computer is used to receive, hold and distribute messages among participants' computers.

COMPUTER VIRUS A "rogue" computer program designed to replicate itself in the memory or storage devices of other computers.

(THE) CONFERENCE BOARD OF CANADA The Conference Board of Canada is an independent, not-for-profit research organization with affiliates in the United States and Europe. Its mission is to help its members anticipate and respond to the increasingly changing global economy.

CONSTRUCTIVIST LEARNING (Construction) A process of creating meaning in which learners are actively engaged in analyzing their own perspectives, organizing information and developing their own interpretations. Learners interact with each other and with actual, complex, real-world environments to construct a personal knowledge framework.

DAISY CHAIN The sequential linking of microphones in the AL or AGL context where the first is connected to the second, which is connected to the third, and so on, as opposed to all the microphones being linked to one central source.

DELAYED-TIME (see also ASYNCHRONOUS) Learners and instructors are not linked at the same time. The originators of messages create and send the messages at a time convenient to them; the messages are stored until the recipients find it convenient to retrieve them. Letters, voice-mail messages and e-mail are all examples of delayed-time communication.

DESKTOP SOLUTIONS Term used to describe information and communications technologies that can operate on the home or office "desktop" computer.

DIGITAL Information contained in the form of zeros (0) and ones (1) for transmission. Digital information formats may include video, audio, graphics and text.

DISTANCE EDUCATION (see also OPEN LEARNING) Educational opportunities that are made available to students who are separated by place and/or time from the institution offering the learning opportunities. Communication between learners and instructors and/or among learners occurs through technology such as print, computers, television or telephone. Some face-to-face contact may also occur.

DOCUMENT SCANNER Equipment that resembles a photocopier in that pictures or pieces of paper are put on a clear piece of glass or plastic and scanned by a light source. Photocopiers are designed to reproduce the material on a piece of paper; document scanners convert the material into a digital signal so that it can be entered into a computer and reproduced on a computer screen.

DOWNLOAD (see also UPLOAD) The process of copying a file from a remote computer to one's own computer. The process uses a protocol (usually File Transfer Protocol) to guarantee that the transfer is error-free and arrives in exactly the same format as it is stored on the remote computer.

E-MAIL (ELECTRONIC MAIL) The exchange of textual and nontextual messages from one computer to another using software packages designed to store and forward messages received or sent.

EMOTICONS Keyboard characters used to indicate humor, emphasis and other emotions and reactions that we usually obtain from voice or gestures.

ERGONOMICS The study of how humans interact physically with machines and environments.

GROUP AUDIO TERMINAL (see also SPEAKERPHONE) A telephone that can be used by an individual or a group of learners at home, in the workplace or in a seminar or classroom environment.

GROUPWARE Computer software that creates audio and audiographic conferencing environments through a desktop computer, rather than through telephones, speakerphones or specialized graphics equipment.

HOLISTIC APPROACH An approach that acknowledges the interconnectedness of reality and the concept of wholeness, rather than fragmentation. In education, holistic methods recognize that we are physical, psychological, affiliative, spiritual and economic beings.

HYPERLINKS Words that are specially tagged by HTML in a WWW document to create links to other WWW resources.

HYPERTEXT MARKUP LANGUAGE (HTML) The protocol used to create documents for publication and distribution on the World Wide Web. HTML consists of tags added to text documents that format and create links to other WWW resources.

ICONS Drawings or symbols that appear on the screen and that allow you to perform various functions on the computer.

INFORMATION HIGHWAY The term used to describe once-separate telephone and television communications networks and computing systems that are converging into a single global network of networks.

INFORMATION LITERACY The ability to use print and multimedia indexing tools and resources to access relevant information efficiently in formal and informal settings such as the library or the home.

INTERNET A worldwide collection of computer networks. The networks use a commun communications protocol and addressing scheme to share resources with one another. Owned by no one, it is maintained collectively by the individual national, regional, commercial and institutional networks that make up the Internet. It is a learning, information and business tool.

INTERNET SERVICE PROVIDER (ISP) A company or institution that provides Internet connection to any user willing to pay the stated fee. An ISP will provide you with an e-mail address and connectivity software, as well as access to the Internet through a bank of modems and telephone numbers you call.

INTRANET (**see also LAN and WAN**) A network of servers and computers or workstations within a single company or organization that uses Internet protocols and programs.

LISTSERV The software that manages electronic discussion groups or computer conference distribution lists. These discussion groups are often called lists. Once a person's electronic address is on a list, he or she can send or receive a message. LISTSERV sends a message from one person directly to everyone else on the list.

LOCAL AREA NETWORK (LAN) (**see also INTRANET and WAN**) A network (usually high-speed) that connects computers and other communications devices inside a single building or throughout a group of buildings that are close to one another such as a campus.

LOG ON Computer jargon for accessing your e-mail or other services on your computer.

LURKER A person who reads or "listens to" a chat line or course discussion without actively participating in the discussion. Lurking is encouraged for newcomers to a group, but is discouraged in learning environments on the practical grounds that learning does not occur effectively without participation, and on the ethical grounds that "all take and no give" is not fair.

META-LEARNING STRATEGIES Self-reflective and self-managing strategies that enable us to assess the effectiveness of how we learn, as distinct from assessing whether we have learned what we intended to learn.

MODEL A generalized and structured way of seeing events and processes that helps us clarify our values and outlooks, see linkages between concepts and events, predict likely results, figure out alternative solutions to problems and compare what they can do with what they might do.

MODEM A piece of equipment that typically converts the digital signals internal to a computer into analog signals that can be transported over ordinary telephone lines. A modem can be inside the computer and so invisible to the user, or it can be a visible piece of equipment outside of the computer. Modems are often defined by the highest speed at which they can transmit and receive data. Common speed formats, measured in kilobits per second (Kbps), are 14.4 and 28.8.

MULTI-USER DOMAIN (MUD) A text-based virtual-reality program in which users interact in real-time as they move between different rooms in an environment.

MULTI-USER OBJECT ORIENTED (MOO) A newer version of the MUD, it allows users to create characters, objects and rooms for text-based virtual-reality sites.

NETWORKED LEARNING (NL) Learning that happens when learners and instructors use computers to exchange messages, engage in dialogue and access resources as part of a learning endeavor. Interaction can occur in real-time, when learners and instructors are all present at the same time, or in delayed-time, when they are not linked at the same time.

OFF-LINE Work that is done when the user is not connected to the Internet or an Intranet. The product of this work is often shared with others at a later time.

ON-LINE Work that is done when the user is connected to the Internet or an Intranet.

OPEN LEARNING An instructional system that places many aspects of the learning process under the control of the learner so that she or he can choose when and how to study.

PARADIGM A world view. The way in which an individual or society organizes and values its actions. A paradigm is based on beliefs and expectations.

PEDAGOGY The science, art and practice of teaching and learning. From the Greek, "to lead a child." Literally, it refers to the teaching of children; andragogy should be used to refer to teaching adults. Pedagogy is often used loosely to refer to teaching both adults and children.

PLAIN OLD TELEPHONE SERVICE (POTS) The basic (analog) telephone set, linked by copper wires.

PROTOCOL An agreed-upon set of rules that govern the format, timing and error control of transmissions on a network so that networks can communicate with one another.

PSYCHOMOTOR DOMAIN (see also AFFECTIVE DOMAIN and COGNITIVE DOMAIN) The third of three domains that form a hierarchy or taxonomy of educational objectives. This domain refers to operational skills and the physical movements and controls that characterize each skill category. Objectives in this domain usually include related thinking (Cognitive Domain) and feeling (Affective Domain) aspects.

SCREEN-WRAP Software that ensures that text is displayed on a computer screen within the horizontal edges of the monitor. You may have to move down the screen to read a long message, but you do not have to continue to move sideways.

SEARCH ENGINE (see also BROWSER) A computer program that allows users to enter key words and be linked to materials on the Internet, an Intranet or a single computer system.

SERVER A software program that runs on a "central" computer connected to the Internet. It manages the linkages among remote computers and permits activities such as e-mail, BBS, LISTSERV, delayed or simultaneous discussions and resource searching.

SPEAKERPHONE (see also GROUP AUDIO TERMINAL) A telephone the can be used by an individual or a group of learners at home, in the workplace or in a seminar or classroom environment. A microphone in the speakerphone transmits people's voices and a loudspeaker amplifies them.

STENTOR More properly called The Stentor Alliance, Stentor is a consortium of Canada's full-service telecommunications companies and their holding companies.

SYNCHRONOUS Taking place at the same time (in real-time). For example, talking with someone on the telephone could be described as "synchronous communication."

TAXONOMY An ordered classification system based on a hierarchy of levels that contains general and specific categories of learning objectives (or, in other disciplines, of plants and animals).

TRANSFER CONTROL PROTOCOL/INTERNET PROTOCOL (TCP/IP) The software protocol used to link computers on the Internet.

TWISTED COPPER PAIR A telephone line. Copper has been the standard for telephone lines since before the turn of the century, as it is a better conductor of electricity than other metals. A telephone line comprises two wires: a grounded wire that is twisted around another wire that carries the signal.

UPLOAD (see also DOWNLOAD) To send a file from one computer to a remote computer, which other users then access to retrieve the file.

VIDEOCONFERENCE A technical arrangement in which television monitors, cameras and microphones are linked together by a bridge so that people in three or more sites can see, hear and speak to one another.

VIDEO LEARNING See COMPRESSED VIDEO LEARNING.

VIRTUAL REALITY An environment that simulates a real-life context on a computer screen.

VIRUS A computer program designed to replicate itself in the memory or storage devices of other computers; it often has destructive or practical-joke components that can damage materials stored on the infected computer.

WHITEBOARD A white display device that is marked with a dry-erase marker. In the AGL context, a whiteboard is typically a three-by-four-foot electronic display device that can be activated by touch or by an electronic marker. It can be linked by telephone to other such devices so that whatever is written at one site is seen at all other sites.

WIDE AREA NETWORK (WAN) (see also LAN and INTRANET) A network of computers and other communications devices that are located over a large geographic area such as a city, province or state.

WORLD WIDE WEB (WWW) A communication protocol of the Internet that deals with text, audio, video and any other type of format.

Contact Names and Addresses

This section provides the names and addresses of the people whose stories are described in Chapter 4 (listed in the order in which their stories appear in the chapter), those who are quoted elsewhere in this book and the vendors who provided materials. Since space has limited the extent of their discussions, this section provides the information you need to contact them if you wish to pursue issues in more depth.
NOTE: Some of the people we interviewed for Chapter 4 have since moved on to other positions. The names below are appropriate project contacts at the time this manuscript was finalized.

WORKPLACE USERS

Remediation Training in the Financial Sector
TRACY HUTCHEON
Employee Development Centre
CIBC
750 Lawrence Avenue West, E2
Toronto, ON M6A 1B8
Tel.: (416) 784-2333

Vendor-Developed Applications for Video Learning
JOYCE M. MILLICAN
Human Resources Support Manager
NBTel
1 Brunswick Square
P.O. Box 1430
Saint John, NB E2L 4K2
Tel.: (506) 658-7382
Fax: (506) 694-2392

CAROL ANNE FORSGREN
Forsgren & Associates
P.O. Box 6131, Station A
Saint John, NB E2L 4R6
Tel.: (506) 849-5330
Fax: (506) 849-5339
cforsgrn@nbnet.nb.ca

Evaluating Diverse Workplace Applications
LOUIS VALOIS
Personnel Administration
Fisheries and Oceans Canada
Centennial Tower
200 Kent Street
Ottawa, ON K1A 0N7
Tel.: (613) 990-3027
Fax: (613) 991-4982

Taking Video Learning for a Test Drive: Lessons Learned
ELLEN LEDERMAN
Distance Education Coordinator
Senior Education Consultant
Addiction Research Foundation
33 Russell Street
Toronto, ON M5S 2S1
Tel.: (416) 595-6636
Fax: (416) 595-6644
elederma@arf.org

CONSORTIA

Transferring Knowledge in Science and Engineering
MICHAEL CHARLES, PH.D., P.ENG.
Dean, Faculty of Applied Sciences & Engineering
University of Toronto
35 St. George Street, Room 170
Toronto, ON M5S 1A4
Tel.: (416) 978-3131
Fax: (416) 978-4859

SANDRA HODDER
Program Coordinator
School of Computing & Information Management
Sheridan College
1430 Trafalgar Road
Oakville, ON
L6H 2L1
Tel.: (905) 845-9430 ext. 2507
Fax: (905) 815-4035
sandra.hodder@sheri–dan.on.ca

Minimizing Costs in a Transnational Consortium for Graduate Education
JEF VAN DEN BRANDEN
Educational Director
EuroPACE 2000
Celestijnenlaan 200A
3001 Heverlee, Belgium
Tel: +32-16-32 75 73
Fax: +32-16-32 79 95
jef.vandenbranden@europace.be

FORMAL EDUCATION SECTOR

Changing the Mindset: A Pilot Project
STEPHEN OLIVER
Technology Consultant
Central Huron Secondary School
165 Princess Street East
Clinton, ON N0M 1L0
Tel.: (519) 482-3471
Fax: (519) 482-9718
soliver@hookup.net

Meeting the Needs of Stakeholders in Health and Education
JANICE COOPER
Director (A)
Telemedicine Centre
Health Sciences Centre
Memorial University of Newfoundland
St. John's, NF A1B 3V6
Tel.: (709) 737-6654
Fax: (709) 737-7054
jlcooper@morgan.ucs.mun.ca

Offering a Graduate Course in Engineering

IRENA KIREK
Manager
Centre for Distance Learning and Innovative Technologies
The University of Calgary
2500 University Drive NW
Calgary, AB T2N 1N4
Tel.: (403) 220-7346
Fax: (403) 777-1959
IKIREK@acs.ucalgary.ca

Learning from a Mature College Network

PAUL RIXON
Manager
Videoconferencing Services
South Australian Department of Employment
Training and Further Education
Adelaide Institute of Technical and Further Education
20 Light Square, GPO
Box 1872
Adelaide, South Australia, 5001
Tel: +68 8 207-8527
Fax: +61 8 207-8552
paulrix@tafe.sa.edu.au

Customizing Faculty Training Programs

DENIS MAYER
Director
Student Affairs
Laurentian University
Ramsey Lake Road
Sudbury, ON P3E 2C6
Tel.: (705) 675-1151 ext. 3940
Fax: (705) 673-6533
DMAYER@nickel.laurentian.ca

Supporting an Institution's Mission through Video Learning

DIANA M. HENSHAW, D. ED.
Director
Division of Continuing Studies
East Carolina University
Greenville, NC 27858-4353
Tel.: (919) 328-6321
Fax: (919) 328-4350
cehensha@ecuvm.cis.ecu.edu

J. BARRY DUVALL, PH.D.
Department of Industrial Technology
School of Industry and Technology
105 Flanagan
Greenville, NC 27858-4353
Tel.: (919) 328-4661
Fax: (919) 328–1618
itduvall@homer.sit.ecu.edu

RONALD ROUSE
Chief Communications Engineer
East Carolina University School of Medicine
Center for Health Sciences Communication
Broady Building, Room 15-10
Greenville, NC 27834
Tel.: (919) 816-2136
Fax: (919) 816-2495
ron@sparky.med.ecu.edu

MINORITY CULTURES AND SPECIAL NEEDS APPLICATIONS

Serving Special Needs Learners through Desktop Video Learning

RON KLASSEN
Market Manager
Signature Service Centre
Stentor Resource Centre Inc.
410-22nd Street East, 5th Floor
Saskatoon, SK S7K 1W8
Tel.: (306) 931-5633
Fax: (306) 931-5459
ron.klassen@sasktel.sk.ca

SUSAN ALCORN MACKAY
Director
Special Needs Regional Resource Centre
Cambrian College
Sudbury, ON
Tel.: (705) 566-8101 ext. 7793
Fax: (705) 524-7329
samackay@venus.cambrianc.on.ca

ROLF POLAN
Marion M. Graham Collegiate
602 Lenore Drive
Saskatoon, SK S7K 5A6
Tel.: (306) 683-7750
Fax: (306) 683-7777

Serving Aboriginal Learners through the Virtual Institution Model

KAYAS Cultural College
Box 1830
High Level, AB T0H 1Z0
Tel.: (403) 759-2030
Fax: (403) 759-2021

Serving the Needs of Francophone Learners

RÉAL SAMSON, PH.D.
President
Le Collège de l'Acadie
P.O. Box 8
La Butte, NS B0W 2L0
Tel.: (902) 769-0851
Fax: (902) 769-0165

MICHAEL J. JEFFREY
Director
Learning Resources
& Technology
Department of Education
and Culture
3770 Kempt Road
Halifax, NS B3K 4X8
Tel: (902) 424-2462
Fax: (902) 424-0633
jeffremg@gov.ns.ca

ROBERT MAYRAND
Interim President
Le Collège des Grands Lacs
595 Bay Street, Room 403, Box 42
Toronto, ON M5G 2C2
Tel.: (416) 599-5009
Fax: (416) 599-50269

M. DON MCDONELL
Coordinator
Centre de l'éducation à distance
Services de l'éducation permanente
University of Ottawa
139 Louis Pasteur
Ottawa, ON K1N 6N5
Tel.: (613) 562-5800 ext. 6519
Fax: (613) 562-5947
dmcdonel@aix1.uottawa.ca

EVALUATION CONTACTS

URMIL CHUGH
c/o Centre for Distance Learning and Innovative Technologies
The University of Calgary
2500 University Drive NW
Calgary, AB T2N 1N4
Tel.: (403) 220-7346
Fax: (403) 777-1959

MARGARET HAUGHEY
Professor
Faculty of Education
7-104 Education North
University of Alberta
Edmonton, AB T6G 2G5
Tel.: (403) 492-7609
Fax: (403) 492-2024
margaret.haughey@UAlberta.CA

COLIN LATCHEM
Associate Professor
Head, Teaching & Learning Group
Curtin University
Perth, Western Australia
Tel.: +6 19 351-2587
Fax: +6 19 351–2777
c.latchem@info.curtin.edu.au

OTHERS QUOTED

ROBERT D. CLARK
Manager
Media Services
University College of the Cariboo
P.O. Box 3010
Kamloops, BC V2C 5N3
Tel.: (250) 828-5486
Fax: (250) 828-5483
rclark@cariboo.bc.ca

PAUL D. GUILD
Director
Institute for Innovation Research
Faculty of Engineering
University of Waterloo
Waterloo, ON N2L 3G1
Tel. & Fax: (519) 888-4802
guild@sail.uwaterloo.ca

DAVID SADLEIR
Professor
Department of Industrial Engineering
Faculty of Applied Science and Engineering
University of Toronto
4 Taddle Creek Road
Toronto, ON M5S 1A4
Tel.: (416) 978-5666
Fax: (416) 978-3453

JOHN MITCHELL
Managing Director
John Mitchell & Associates
Level 1, Oxford Corner
169 Unley Road
Unley, South Australia 5061
Tel.: +6 18 373-5201
Fax: +6 18 373-3564
johnm@jma.com.au

CHERE CAMPBELL GIBSON
Associate Professor
Department of Continuing and Vocational Education
University of Wisconsin, Madison
1300 Linden Drive
Madison, WI 53706
Tel.: (608) 262-8611
Fax: (608) 262-5335
cgibson@macc.wisc.edu

JOE GAMBINO
Education Department, Ontario Real Estate Association
929 Duncan Mills Road
Don Mills, ON M3B 1Z2
Tel.: (416) 445-9910
Fax: (416) 445-2644

WILLIAM A. WEIMER
Bridgewater Research Group
34 Windward Drive
Asheville, NC 28803
Tel.: (704) 298-5169
Fax: (704) 298-5186
72772.3307@compuserve.com

CRAIG SCOTT
Professor
Faculty of Law
University of Toronto
78 Queen's Park
Toronto, ON M5S 2C5
Tel.: (416) 978-5611
Fax: (416) 978-2648

CONTRIBUTING VENDORS

BERNIE KOVER
Education & Health Care Sales
ADCOM Inc.
310 Judson Street, Unit 5
Toronto, ON M8Z 5T6
Tel.: (416) 251-3355
Fax: (416) 251-3977

SHERRY PILLOW
Customer Relations Representative
VTEL Corporation
108 Wild Basin Road
Austin, TX 78746
Tel.: (512) 437-2266
Fax: (512) 437-2718

MARIAN LEVY
Vice-President, Marketing
Tandberg Canada Inc.
175 Montpellier
Montréal, QC H2N 2G5
Tel.: (514) 748-5224 ext. 6409
Fax: (514) 748-5229